Law E

EVIDENCE

3rd edition

James Chalmers

Senior Lecturer in Law, University of Edinburgh

DUNDEE UNIVERSITY PRESS
2012

First edition published in Great Britain in 2006 by
Dundee University Press
University of Dundee
Dundee DD1 4HN

www.dup.dundee.ac.uk

Reprinted 2007, 2008
Second edition published 2009
Third edition published 2012

ISBN 978 1 84586 135 3

No natural forests were destroyed to make this product; only farmed timber was used
and replanted.

British Library Cataloguing-in-Publication Data
A catalogue record for this book is available on request from the British Library

Typeset by Waverley Typesetters, Warham
Printed and bound by Bell & Bain Ltd, Glasgow

CONTENTS

TABLE OF CASES

TABLE OF STATUTES

Page

1 INTRODUCTION AND OVERVIEW

Evidence is that branch of the law which regulates how issues may be proved in court. It establishes the sources and methods which a court may use in order to find that facts have – or have not – been proven, and thereby decide cases.

ADMISSIBILITY OF EVIDENCE

Much of the law of evidence is concerned with the kind of evidence which can legitimately be put before a court and taken into account in decision-making.

If evidence is to be admissible, two things are required. First, it must be *relevant*. Secondly, its use must not be prohibited by an *exclusionary rule*.

Relevance

Defining relevance is not an easy task. The leading textbook on the law of evidence suggests simply that in "very general terms relevant evidence may be said to be evidence which is logically connected with those matters in dispute between the parties" (*Walkers on Evidence* (3rd edn, 2009), para 1.3.1). Another way of putting it is that evidence is relevant if it tends to show that one of the facts in issue is more probable, or less probable.

In a trial for murder, for example, it might be relevant to show that the accused was seen near the place where the victim's body was found, shortly before the body was discovered; that he was seen covered in blood shortly after the event; or that he was seen burning his clothes in his back garden that evening. All of those facts might, applying normal processes of reasoning, help lead us to the conclusion that the accused did in fact commit the crime. It is important to say "might", because relevance depends entirely on context. All these facts probably would be relevant if the victim had been killed in a frenzied attack with a knife, and was discovered shortly after death occurred. If he had been killed by poisoning and his body had lain undiscovered for a week, it may be that none of these facts would be relevant.

By the same token, if the murder victim were the husband of the accused's lover, or someone to whom the accused owed money as a result of gambling debts, it might be relevant to show that the accused was an adulterer or a compulsive gambler. If not, the relevance of those facts would be in serious doubt. This merely demonstrates how any attempt to say, in the abstract, that one or another piece of evidence is "relevant" or "irrelevant" is most likely doomed to failure.

We can, however, usefully distinguish between two types of relevance – *direct* and *indirect*. Direct evidence is evidence of the fact in issue itself. Indirect evidence is that which, although not evidence of the thing itself, might lead – or help lead – us to the conclusion that the fact has or has not been proven. So, to continue with the murder example, the testimony of the eyewitness who saw the accused stab the victim is direct evidence of guilt. Evidence that the accused was seen running away from the scene of the crime merely produces one link in a chain of inferences leading to the conclusion that the accused stabbed the victim.

Both the Crown and the defence, in a criminal trial, may wish to prove a fact. Just as the Crown may adduce direct or indirect evidence of guilt, so the accused may adduce direct or indirect evidence of innocence. The accused might elicit direct evidence of innocence from an eyewitness who says that she saw someone other than the accused stab the victim, or indirect evidence of innocence from a witness who testifies that the accused was a keen runner who often went on training runs past the scene of the crime.

Naturally, witnesses in a trial may mention many facts which are, strictly speaking, irrelevant. Provided, however, that court time is not unduly wasted, and none of the parties objects, it may not be necessary strictly to enforce the requirement of relevance. It is, nevertheless, absolutely fundamental to the law of evidence.

Even if evidence is relevant, it may still be inadmissible, on the basis that it falls foul of one of the *exclusionary rules* of the law of evidence.

The exclusionary rules

If evidence is relevant, why not allow it to be led in court? A number of reasons might be suggested. These are not rules *in themselves*, but only reasons which might be offered to justify the various exclusionary rules. Some of these rules can be justified for a combination of these reasons, rather than a single one. Equally, some of these justifications might be contested, and the arguments presented here are unlikely to be universally accepted.

- It is *not the best evidence*. For example, the law generally excludes "hearsay" evidence (see Chapter 5). As a rule, if A is charged with murdering B, it is not competent to call C to testify that he heard D say that he (D) saw A commit the crime. If anyone is to be called to testify to this, it should be D. But, of course, there may be circumstances in which this is not possible – perhaps D is dead – and C's evidence might then become admissible. There is also a rule – termed the "best evidence" rule (see Chapter 6) – which applies to real and documentary evidence, for similar reasons.

- It is *unreliable*. This is, for example, another reason for excluding hearsay evidence. In the above example, D's evidence has not been given on oath in a court of law. It is not subject to cross-examination, and the judge and jury are not able to observe his demeanour as he gives evidence. For reasons such as this, his evidence might be argued to be too unreliable to be used. However, the law now generally allows hearsay evidence to be used when it is the best evidence available in criminal cases. In civil cases, the rule against hearsay has been abolished by statute. There is, as Chapter 5 notes, a tension between excluding hearsay because it is not the best evidence, or because it is inherently unreliable – approaches which, in some cases, lead to different results.

- It is *misleading*. If A is charged with murdering B, we might think it relevant that he has committed previous crimes of violence. But we might also be worried that a jury would attach too much weight to this evidence, and fail to consider whether it has been specifically proven that he is guilty of the crime charged. For that reason, the law places restrictions on the extent to which evidence of A's "previous misconduct" or "character" can be used against him (see Chapter 9). For similar reasons, where sexual offences are charged, the law restricts the use which can be made of the "sexual history" of the complainer (the alleged victim) in evidence.

- It would be *against public policy* to allow the evidence to be led. For example, it is considered to be particularly important to maintain the confidentiality of the relationship between a solicitor and a client, and so evidence of solicitor–client communications is normally regarded as privileged and so inadmissible (see Chapter 10). This might also be a reason for refusing to allow "improperly obtained" evidence to be admitted (Chapter 8).

- It is *unnecessary*. An example of this is the rule against leading evidence of matters which are within "judicial knowledge" (see Chapter 12). If a witness says that an event took place on Christmas Day, there is no need to lead further evidence to prove that Christmas Day is 25 December. Leading such evidence would be a waste of court time. The rule against hearsay might also be partly justified on a similar basis. If it did not exist, it would be competent to lead evidence not only from D, who saw the murder, but also from E, F, G and H who heard him talk about it in the pub afterwards – and, again, that would be unhelpful and a waste of court time.

For reasons such as these, the law has developed a series of exclusionary rules.

OPINION EVIDENCE

A further exclusionary rule, addressed in Chapter 11, relates to opinion evidence. Normally, witnesses must give evidence of facts, and not of their opinions, and so "opinion evidence" is generally inadmissible. There are, however, circumstances in which such evidence is permitted.

Discussions of the principal exclusionary rules form the bulk of this book. It is not, however, solely concerned with these rules, and considers other issues, as follows:

METHODS OF PROOF: BURDEN, STANDARD, SUFFICIENCY AND PRESUMPTIONS

The following key issues are discussed:

- The *burden* of proof: where a fact is in dispute in a case, which of the parties is required to prove it?
- The *standard* of proof: where a party bears the burden of proof, to what "standard" must they discharge that? Must they prove their case "beyond reasonable doubt", or simply "on the balance of probabilities"?
- *Sufficiency* of proof. In criminal cases, an accused cannot normally be found guilty except on the basis of *corroborated evidence* – that is, evidence from at least two different sources in respect of every crucial fact. Anything less is insufficient for a conviction.

The use of presumptions – specific legal rules by which certain facts (presumed facts) may be inferred from proof of other facts (basic facts) – is considered in Chapter 3.

METHODS OF PROOF: THE COURSE OF A TRIAL OR PROOF

This book also notes the normal course of a trial or proof (Chapter 16) and rules regarding "specialities of witnesses" (Chapter 15) – that is, certain witnesses who are not permitted to give evidence in court, cannot be compelled to do so, or are entitled to the benefit of special rules when giving evidence. Chapter 13 notes how facts may be "admitted" by the parties to a case, thus removing the need for proof.

TERMINOLOGY: ORAL, REAL AND DOCUMENTARY EVIDENCE

Finally, it should be noted that a distinction can be drawn between these three types of evidence, and that this book assumes an understanding of this terminology:

- *"oral" evidence* – that given orally by a witness in court;
- *"real" evidence* – a thing or an item, lodged as a "production" in court. It is normally necessary for a witness to "speak to" (that is, refer to) the item in oral evidence for the real evidence itself to become evidence that the court can take into account;
- *"documentary" evidence* – documents which are lodged in court as productions. Like real evidence, they should normally be spoken to by a witness to become evidence themselves.

Some of the rules discussed in this book apply only to certain specified types of evidence, such as, most obviously, the rules on the admissibility of improperly obtained real and documentary evidence. Where this is the case, it is made clear in the relevant chapter.

CIVIL AND CRIMINAL CASES

The law of evidence is not identical across civil and criminal cases, and stricter standards are frequently applied in the criminal courts, partly because of the public interest in safeguarding accused persons against wrongful conviction. So, for example, the corroboration requirement and the rule against hearsay have now been abolished in respect of civil cases, but remain crucial aspects of the law of criminal evidence. Where the law differs between civil and criminal cases, the differences are set out in the relevant chapter.

In criminal cases, procedural differences between *solemn* and *summary* procedure are also important. Solemn procedure is where the court sits with a jury (or will sit with a jury if and when the case goes to trial); summary procedure is where no jury is involved but the case is decided by a judge sitting alone. While the same rules of evidence apply in both types of case, procedural rules differ and these are noted where relevant.

Essential Facts

- Evidence must be *relevant* in order to be admissible in court.
- Even where evidence is relevant, it may be inadmissible because of an *exclusionary rule*.
- Exclusionary rules can be justified for a number of different reasons, of which some of the most important are that the excluded evidence is (a) not the best evidence available; (b) unreliable; (c) misleading; (d) that it would be against public policy to admit it; or (e) that it is unnecessary.
- The rules of evidence may – and frequently do – differ between civil and criminal cases.

2 BURDENS AND STANDARDS OF PROOF

Two related questions are addressed in this chapter: first, where facts are in dispute, who is required to prove them – who bears the burden of proof? Secondly, where a party bears that burden, to what standard must he discharge it?

THE TYPES OF BURDEN OF PROOF

There are said to be three "types" of burden of proof, as follows:

The "persuasive" or "legal" burden. This is the most important of the three, and as such is often referred to simply as "the burden of proof" rather than as a particular type of burden. This burden rests on the party who must satisfy the court on a particular issue in order for the relevant fact (or facts) to be found proven. Depending on the case, it is possible for different parties to bear persuasive burdens in respect of different issues. For example, where an accused pleads insanity, the prosecution bears the persuasive burden in respect of proving that he has committed the crime, but the accused bears the persuasive burden in respect of proving his plea of insanity. (This is an exception to the normal rule that the burden of proof in a criminal case always rests on the prosecution: see p 10.)

The "evidential" burden. Where an evidential burden is imposed, it requires only that a party identifies sufficient evidence to justify the court considering the issue as a live one. That might be evidence adduced by that party, but it need not be – they could point to evidence adduced by another party to that effect.

In practice, the evidential burden is of most importance in criminal cases, where the accused will frequently bear an evidential burden in respect of certain defences, but the prosecution will bear the legal burden of disproving that defence beyond a reasonable doubt. This preserves the presumption of innocence, but avoids the prosecution having to start from the position of disproving all sorts of hypothetical and fanciful defences. So, for example, an accused who wishes to rely on the defence of self-defence must be able to point to some evidence supporting this claim (the evidential burden). But provided he can meet this minimal requirement, it is then for the prosecution to disprove his claim (the legal burden) –

which must be done beyond a reasonable doubt (the relevant standard of proof). (See *Lambie* v *HM Advocate* (1973).)

The "provisional" or "tactical" burden. This is not, strictly speaking, any sort of legal rule at all and may be more confusing than helpful. The term is sometimes used to refer to the situation where the party bearing the *legal* burden has led sufficiently strong evidence in support of their case so that, in a practical sense, the other party will find it necessary to lead contrary evidence in order to avoid losing the case. In such a situation, that other party may be said to bear a "tactical" burden. This does not mean, however, that the burden of proof shifts to the accused. In *Tallis* v *HM Advocate* (1982), where the appeal court was highly critical of a sheriff's direction to the jury which suggested this could happen:

> "the sheriff severed the last link in the chain of impartiality required of him by giving to the jury what appears to us to be a serious misdirection in law. He said this: 'Though the situation may arise, ladies and gentlemen, that the Crown puts forward such a strong case that it is only if you are satisfied with the explanation given by the accused, that you would be entitled to acquit him and again that may very well be the situation here you feel ...' The gravity of this misdirection lies in the plain indication to the jury that in certain circumstances the onus of proof shifts to the accused ...".

A jury, considering the case after all the evidence has been led, must be directed by reference to the *legal* burden of proof, not the *provisional* one. The "provisional burden" may be a useful way of describing the position that may arise midway through a case, but it is not a legal rule that assists in determining the outcome of a case. As Wilkinson has observed, given that "the provisional onus [burden] never arises as a matter of law, it may be questioned whether it is necessary to use the term at all" (*The Scottish Law of Evidence* (1986), p 181). There are, however, two specifically recognised instances where a provisional burden falls on the accused, as follows:

The doctrine of recent possession

In certain circumstances, the fact that the accused is found in "recent possession" of stolen goods may cast a provisional burden on him to prove that he is not in fact guilty of theft or reset. The conditions have been set out as follows:

"If the rule is to have full effect in shifting the onus from the prosecution to the accused and raising a presumption of guilt which the accused must redargue or fail, three conditions must concur:– (a) that the stolen goods should be found in the possession of the accused; (b) that the interval between the theft of the goods and their discovery in the accused's possession should be short ... and (c) that there should be 'other criminative circumstances' over and above the bare fact of possession."

(*Fox* v *Paterson* (1948), per the Lord Justice-General (Cooper) at 108)

The reference to the onus of proof shifting may be unfortunate, although it has been repeated by the courts since (see, eg, *Cryans* v *Nixon* (1955)) and the appeal court has suggested that the doctrine of recent possession "cannot be confined within the ordinary rule that the onus of proof remains throughout on the Crown" (*McDonald* v *HM Advocate* (1990), per the Lord Justice-General (Hope) at 44). In principle, the legal burden rests with the prosecution but can be discharged by proof of "recent possession" in this way, and in such circumstances all that shifts is the "provisional" burden.

Facts peculiarly within the knowledge of the accused

The courts have recognised that, where an explanation for otherwise suspicious conduct lies peculiarly within the knowledge of the accused, a provisional burden may fall upon him to explain his conduct. In *HM Advocate* v *Hardy* (1938), the accused was charged with having committed fraud by pretending to be the husband of a deceased woman and as such entitled to legal rights in her estate. In charging the jury, the trial judge (Lord Justice-Clerk Aitchison) noted that the accused had not gone into the witness-box to say where he had met the deceased, where they were married, or what had happened to the men he claimed had acted as witnesses at the ceremony. He went on to say (at 147):

"there are certain cases in which the proved facts may raise a presumption of guilt, and in which, in the absence of some explanation by the person accused, – where the person accused is the one person who can know the real truth – a jury may be entitled to proceed to draw an inference of guilt; and I direct you in law that this is one of them".

This might, at first sight, be thought to conflict with the right to silence. An answer to this "conflict" is suggested by *Mochan* v *Herron* (1972), where Sheriff Peterson observed that an accused in suspicious circumstances was fully entitled to remain silent (unlike other witnesses, who can be held in contempt of court for not testifying) – but if the accused did remain silent there could be no objection to the court drawing its own conclusion from the evidence before it.

WHO BEARS THE BURDEN OF PROOF?

Criminal cases

In criminal cases, the basic rule is that the burden of proof rests with the prosecution:

> "the jury was told that what is familiarly known as the presumption of innocence in criminal cases applied to the appellant (in light of his ambiguous character) with less effect than it would have applied to a man whose character was not open to suspicion. This amounted, in our opinion, to a clear misdirection in law. The presumption of innocence applies to every person charged with a criminal offence in precisely the same way, and it can be overcome only by evidence relevant to prove the crime with the commission of which he is charged". (*Slater* v *HM Advocate* (1928), per the Lord Justice-General (Clyde) at 105)

At one time, it was thought that the accused was required to prove certain defences (such as self-defence) which are referred to as "special defences". It was confirmed in *Lambie* v *HM Advocate* (1973) that this is *not* the case. The accused must give advance notice of his intention to raise a special defence, and bears the evidential burden – in that he must be able to point to some evidence raising the defence as an issue – but provided he has met these minimal requirements, it is for the prosecution to disprove the defence beyond a reasonable doubt.

Special defences impose a requirement on the accused to provide advance notice that he intends to rely on the defence, but (with an exception noted in the next paragraph) they do not shift the burden of proof. At common law, the special defences are alibi, incrimination, insanity and self-defence. By statute, automatism, coercion and consent in sexual offences are to be treated as if they were special defences. All these defences must be notified before trial in both solemn and summary procedure (for the specific procedural rules, see ss 78 and 149B of the Criminal Procedure (Scotland) Act 1995).

Common law exceptions

At common law, there are two defences which place a burden of proof on the accused. These are insanity and diminished responsibility. (The first is a special defence but the latter is not, as it does not result in the acquittal of the accused, but merely reduces a charge of murder to culpable homicide.) It is sometimes said that these defences are exceptional because of the "presumption of sanity" but that is just another way of stating the rule. A better explanation is that these are defences which it would be particularly difficult for the prosecution to disprove – particularly without any power to force the accused to submit to a psychiatric examination – and so the burden is placed on the accused for reasons of convenience as much as anything else. Section 168 of the Criminal Justice and Licensing (Scotland) Act 2010 puts both of these defences in statutory form. The term "insanity" is not used in the Act, where the defence is given no name and the relevant section is headed "Criminal responsibility of persons with mental disorder". The Act does not alter the burden of proof in respect of these defences.

Statutory exceptions

Although there are only two common law exceptions to the rule that the burden of proof rests with the prosecution, it is open to Parliament to place the burden of proof on the defence by way of legislation. This may be done in relation to defences to specific crimes. An example is s 47(1) of the Criminal Law (Consolidation) (Scotland) Act 1995, which provides that "Any person who without lawful authority or reasonable excuse, the proof whereof shall lie on him, has with him in any public place any offensive weapon shall be guilty of an offence".

It is, however, relatively unusual for a statute to make express provision as to where the burden of proof lies. There is a general provision in the Criminal Procedure (Scotland) Act 1995 as follows:

> "Where, in relation to an offence created by or under an enactment any exception, exemption, proviso, excuse, or qualification, is expressed to have effect whether by the same or any other enactment, the exception, exemption, proviso, excuse or qualification need not be specified or negatived in the indictment or complaint, and the prosecution is not required to prove it, but the accused may do so." (Criminal Procedure (Scotland) Act 1995, Sch 3, para 16)

This means that in order to determine where the burden of proof lies, it is necessary to decide whether the "defence" pled by the accused is an "exception, exemption, proviso, excuse or qualification", or its absence is an "integral part of the offence" (see Sheriff Gordon's commentary to *Earnshaw* v *HM Advocate* (1981)). If it is the latter, it is for the prosecution to prove its absence – if the former, the accused bears the persuasive burden of proving that the defence is made out. This is a question of statutory interpretation which will vary from case to case.

Normally the burden placed on the accused will be a persuasive burden, but in some cases a persuasive burden may be regarded as contrary to the presumption of innocence which is guaranteed under Art 6(2) of the European Convention on Human Rights. The European Court has considered reverse burdens to be unobjectionable so long as they are confined within "reasonable limits" (*Salabiaku* v *France* (1991)), and the House of Lords has more recently said that reverse burdens are legitimate so long as they are kept within reasonable limits and are not arbitrary (*Sheldrake* v *DPP* (2005)), where Lord Bingham sets out at para 21 a list of factors to be taken into account in making that assessment). Where the courts consider that a persuasive burden would violate the presumption of innocence, they may read the statute as imposing only an evidential burden on the accused. Such a burden does not violate the Art 6(2) right (*R* v *DPP, ex parte Kebilene* (2000), per Lord Hope of Craighead at 379).

Where the accused bears the persuasive burden, he is not required to lead corroborated evidence in order to discharge it (*King* v *Lees* (1993)). (This is in contrast to the rule which requires that the Crown lead corroborated evidence in order to secure a conviction: see Chapter 4.)

Civil cases

It is often said that, in civil cases, the burden of proof "rests with the party who would fail if no evidence were adduced on either side" (Dickson, *A Treatise on the Law of Evidence in Scotland* (3rd edn, 1887), para 25), a passage repeatedly cited by other writers). This is accurate but not always helpful – without knowing where the burden of proof lies, it is difficult to see how this party could be identified.

More usefully, it has been said that "he who asserts a right given to him by the law must prove the facts necessary to establish it" (Wilkinson, *The Scottish Law of Evidence* (1986), p 182). This means that the burden of proof will normally rest with the pursuer.

It is possible, however, for the burden to be borne by different parties in respect of different issues. For example, in an action in delict based on negligence, the pursuer will normally bear the burden of showing that the defender has been negligent. If the defender wishes to plead a defence such as contributory negligence, or *volenti non fit iniuria*, then he will bear the burden of proof in respect of that issue. This is because a party to a civil case will not normally be required to prove a negative – and so it is for the defender to prove these defences, not for the pursuer to disprove them.

Statutory provisions may alter the burden of proof in certain cases. *Nimmo* v *Alexander Cowan & Sons Ltd* (1967) is usually regarded as the leading case on the subject, although it is really only illustrative, as the case turned on the wording of the particular statute under consideration. *Nimmo* concerned the alleged breach of a statutory duty requiring that premises "shall, so far as is reasonably practicable, be made and kept safe for any person working there" (Factories Act 1961, s 29(1)). It was held that it was for the pursuer to prove that the premises were not safe, but not that it was not "reasonably practicable" to make them safe. If the defender wished to rely upon this proviso, he bore the burden of proof in that respect. In the words of Lord Wilberforce (at 109) "exceptions, etc., are to be set up by those who rely on them".

THE TYPES OF STANDARD OF PROOF

Where a party bears a legal burden of proof, this leads to the question of what *standard* of proof he is required to meet. Scots law recognises only two types of standard of proof: proof "on the balance of probabilities" and proof "beyond reasonable doubt".

The standard of proof in civil cases

It has sometimes been suggested that certain allegations – particularly allegations of criminal conduct – might require to be proved to a higher standard than would otherwise be the case in a civil court, perhaps some "intermediate" standard between "the balance of probabilities" and "beyond reasonable doubt". There is a long line of authorities which deal with this point, but it has been settled by *Mullan* v *Anderson* (1993), where a Full Bench decided that, even although the civil case under consideration involved an allegation of murder, there was no reason to depart from the normal rule of proof on the balance of probabilities.

There is a statutory exception to this general rule where an application is made to a sheriff to establish grounds of referral to a children's hearing. Where the basis for the application is s 52(2)(i) of the Children (Scotland) Act 1995 – that the child has committed a criminal offence – then "the standard of proof required in criminal proceedings shall apply" (s 68(3)). Additionally, it has been held that if the case is based on an alternative ground of referral, such as the child being "exposed to moral danger", but the basis for this allegation is that the child has committed criminal acts, then the criminal standard of proof still applies (*Constanda* v *M* (1997)). This avoids s 68(3) being circumvented in such cases by framing the application so that it falls under a heading other than s 52(2)(i).

There is also a common law exception where proceedings are brought for breach of interdict – an action which is regarded as quasi-criminal because it can result in imprisonment. There, the standard of proof is "beyond reasonable doubt" (*Gribben* v *Gribben* (1976)).

The standard of proof in criminal cases

In a criminal case, the prosecution is required to prove the guilt of the accused "beyond reasonable doubt". The appeal court has generally been hostile to attempts to define what is meant by this phrase – for example, holding in *Buchanan* v *HM Advocate* (1998) that a sheriff was wrong to define reasonable doubt as the kind of doubt that would "dissuade you from getting married or buying a house". In *A* v *HM Advocate* (2003), the appeal court said (at [12]) that:

> "a trial judge or sheriff adequately fulfils his duty if he tells the jury clearly and concisely that the standard of proof that the Crown is required to meet is proof beyond reasonable doubt and describes the idea of reasonable doubt as one that would cause a juror to hesitate or pause before taking an important decision in the conduct of his own affairs … There is no need, in our opinion, for the trial judge or sheriff to go beyond those directions".

Where a legal burden is placed on the accused, the appropriate standard of proof is the balance of probabilities (*Robertson* v *Watson* (1949)).

Where the Crown has to prove the admissibility of an accused's alleged confession (see Chapter 7), admissibility need be proved only on the balance of probabilities (*Platt* v *HM Advocate* (2004)).

Essential Facts

The concept of burdens of proof

- There are three types of burden of proof: the "persuasive" (or "legal") burden, the "evidential" burden, and the "provisional" (or "tactical") burden.

- The persuasive burden rests on the party who must satisfy the court on a particular issue in order for the relevant fact (or facts) to be found proven.

- In some cases, different parties may bear the persuasive burden in respect of different issues.

- The evidential burden is one which requires a party to identify sufficient evidence to justify an issue being considered – but not to satisfy the court that their contention on that issue is correct.

- In criminal cases, the accused bears an evidential burden to show that certain defences should be considered, but where the accused satisfies that burden, the prosecution then bears the provisional burden of disproving the defence.

- The provisional burden is not a legal rule as such, but a way of expressing the idea that, once one party has led enough evidence to prove their case, the other party may in a practical sense bear a "burden" to lead contrary evidence in order to avoid losing the case.

- The most important example of a provisional burden is where an accused is found in recent possession of stolen goods, in "criminative circumstances". He may then bear a "provisional burden" to prove that he is not guilty of theft or reset.

Who bears the burden of proof?

- In criminal cases, the basic rule is that the burden of proof rests on the prosecution.

- The only common law exceptions to this rule are the defences of insanity and diminished responsibility, which must be proved by the defence. However, the defence need only prove these to the "balance of probabilities" standard.

- Statutory provisions may place a burden of proof on the defence in criminal cases. These "reverse burdens" are subject to scrutiny under Art 6(2) of the European Convention on Human Rights but are permitted as long as they are kept within reasonable limits and are not arbitrary.

- In civil cases, the burden of proof can be said to lie with the party who is asserting a legal right, who must then prove the facts necessary to establish that right. The burden of proof in a civil case can be altered by statute.

Standard of proof

- Scots law recognises only two types of standard of proof: proof "on the balance of probabilities" and proof "beyond reasonable doubt".

- In civil proceedings, the standard of proof is the balance of probabilities even where allegations of criminality are involved. There are, however, exceptions to this rule where a sheriff is asked to consider whether a child can be referred to a children's hearing on the ground that they have committed a criminal offence, or where proceedings are brought for breach of interdict. In those cases, proof beyond reasonable doubt is required.

- In criminal proceedings, the prosecution must prove the accused's guilt beyond reasonable doubt.
- Where the accused bears a persuasive burden in criminal proceedings, the appropriate standard is the balance of probabilities.

Essential Cases

A v HM Advocate (2003): "reasonable doubt" is a doubt "that would cause a juror to hesitate or pause before taking an important decision in the conduct of his own affairs".

Fox v Paterson (1948): where an accused is found in "recent possession" of stolen goods, in "criminative circumstances", this may give rise to a "presumption of guilt" of theft or reset.

Mullan v Anderson (1993): the standard of proof in civil proceedings is proof on the balance of probabilities, even where the case involves an allegation that a person has committed a crime.

Sheldrake v DPP (2005): "reverse burdens" are compatible with the European Convention on Human Rights provided they are kept within reasonable limits and are not arbitrary.

Slater v HM Advocate (1928): the presumption of innocence applies to everyone charged with a criminal offence, regardless of their character.

Tallis v HM Advocate (1982): the burden of proof in a criminal case cannot shift from the prosecution to the defence.

3 PRESUMPTIONS

Presumptions, properly so called, involve certain inferences being drawn from other facts which have been proved or admitted. They involve what may be referred to as a *basic fact* (or facts) and a *presumed fact* (or facts). The existence of the presumed fact is inferred from the proof or admission of the basic fact.

Presumptions are commonly divided into three categories:

- irrebuttable presumptions of law;
- rebuttable presumptions of law;
- rebuttable presumptions of fact.

The language of "presumption" is also sometimes used to restate the burden of proof. For example, reference to the "presumption of innocence" is simply a means of stating that the burden of proof in a criminal trial rests with the prosecution, while the "presumption of sanity" is simply a reference to the rule that a person pleading insanity (or diminished responsibility) as a defence bears the persuasive burden of proving it (see Chapter 2). "Presumptions" in this sense are not discussed further in this chapter.

Irrebuttable presumptions of law

Presumptions of this nature cannot be rebutted by contradictory evidence of any sort. Once the basic fact is admitted or proved, proof of the presumed fact necessarily follows. An example of such a presumption is the statutory rule that "[i]t shall be conclusively presumed that no child under the age of eight years can be guilty of any offence" (Criminal Procedure (Scotland) Act 1995, s 41). Such "presumptions" are probably best understood as substantive rule of law.

Rebuttable presumptions of law and of fact

Where a rebuttable presumption of law applies, proof of the basic fact means that the presumed fact *must* be held established unless the contrary is proved. By contrast, where a rebuttable presumption of fact applies, proof of the basic fact *entitles* – but does not oblige – the court to hold the presumed fact established.

Rebuttable presumptions of law

Rebuttable presumptions of law include the following:

- *Presumptions of survivorship in cases of common calamities.* If two deaths occur in close proximity – usually, but not necessarily, as a result of the same incident – it may be difficult to determine which person died first. The question can be of considerable importance in determining the succession to the deceaseds' estates, and so the matter is now regulated by statutory presumption. Under s 31 of the Succession (Scotland) Act 1964, it is presumed that the younger person survived the older, unless the two persons were spouses or civil partners, in which case it is presumed that neither survived the other.

- *The presumption* omnia rite et solemniter acta praesumuntur: "that everything is done validly and in accordance with the necessary formalities" (*Walkers on Evidence* (3rd edn, 2009), para 3.6.1). This may be referred to simply as a presumption of "regularity and validity". An example of its application is *Sutherland* v *Barbour* (1887), where a feu charter granted 62 years prior to the case coming to court required buildings to be erected in accordance with a plan, but the plan could not be found. The presumption was relied upon in order to hold that the buildings as erected were in compliance with that plan.

- *The presumption against donation.* Where moveable property is transferred from one person to another during the first person's lifetime, there is a strong presumption against this having been a donation (*Grant's Trs* v *McDonald* (1939)).

- *The presumption* pater est quem nuptiae demonstrant (*the father is whom marriage demonstrates*). Under s 5 of the Law Reform (Parent and Child) (Scotland) Act 1986, a man shall be presumed to be the father of a child "if he was married to the mother of the child at any time in the period beginning with the conception and ending with the birth of the child" (s 5(1)(a)), or if both he and the mother have acknowledged that he is the father and he has been registered as such (s 5(1)(b)).

- *A woman aged 53 years or older is presumed to be incapable of child-bearing* (*G's Trs* v *G* (1936)).

This is merely a small selection of the most significant presumptions recognised by the law.

Rebuttable presumptions of fact

Rebuttable presumptions of fact are less easy to identify, probably because it is difficult to differentiate such presumptions from the everyday process of inferring certain facts from other facts where this seems reasonable to do. Indeed, it has been suggested that the distinction between rebuttable presumptions of law and of fact is that the latter are, by definition, not properly recognised by the legal system (*Millar* v *Mitchell, Cadell & Co* (1860) at 844).

Perhaps the best-known example of a rebuttable presumption of fact is *res ipsa loquitur*, a rule of the law of delict which allows an inference of negligence to be drawn where it is shown that the "thing" which caused the accident was under the management of the defendant and should not normally have given rise to such an accident had reasonable care been used:

> "where the thing is shown to be under the management of the defendant or his servants, and the accident is such as in the ordinary course of things does not happen if those who have the management use proper care, it affords reasonable evidence, in the absence of explanation by the defendants, that the accident arose from want of care". (*Scott* v *London & St Katherine's Docks Co* (1865), per Erle CJ at 601, and see *Devine* v *Colvilles Ltd* (1969))

It is also presumed that the possessor of moveable property is the owner (see, eg, *Prangnell-O'Neill* v *Lady Skiffington* (1984)), although the textbooks differ on whether this is properly classed as a rebuttable presumption of law or a rebuttable presumption of fact.

The possession of stolen property in "criminative circumstances" may give rise to a presumption of fact that the possessor is guilty of theft or reset (*Fox* v *Paterson* (1948), discussed in Chapter 2).

Essential Facts

- Presumptions involve a *basic fact* (or facts) and a *presumed fact* (or facts). Where the basic fact is proved or admitted, the presumed fact is held to exist.
- Presumptions take three forms: (i) irrebuttable presumptions of law; (ii) rebuttable presumptions of law; and (iii) rebuttable presumptions of fact.
- Where an *irrebuttable* presumption of *law* applies, the court *must* infer the presumed fact from the basic fact, and this cannot be rebutted by contrary evidence.

- Where a *rebuttable* presumption of *law* applies, the court *must* infer the presumed fact from the basic fact, but the presumed fact may be disproved by contrary evidence.
- Where a *rebuttable* presumption of *fact* applies, the court *may* infer the presumed fact from the basic fact.

4 SUFFICIENCY OF EVIDENCE: THE CORROBORATION RULE

The corroboration rule is one of the most distinctive features of the Scottish law of evidence. At its simplest, it holds that no person may be convicted of a criminal charge on the evidence of a single witness. In the words of Hume:

> "No matter how trivial the offence and how high soever the credit and character of the witness, still our law is averse to rely on his single word, in any inquiry which may affect the person, liberty or fame of his neighbour; and rather than run the risk of such an error, a risk which does not hold when there is a concurrence of testimonies, it is willing that the guilty should escape." (Hume, *Commentaries,* ii, 383)

Although, historically, the requirement applied to civil cases as much as to criminal ones, that is no longer the case. The position in civil cases is noted briefly at the end of this chapter, which is otherwise concerned only with the criminal law.

The scope and meaning of the corroboration rule

The corroboration rule applies to any criminal offence, unless legislation provides otherwise. An example of such legislation is s 21 of the Road Traffic Offenders Act 1988, which states that "the accused may be convicted on the evidence of one witness" in the case of certain specified road traffic offences. Such provisions are, however, relatively unusual.

Where the rule applies, the evidence of two witnesses is essential – but it is not enough in itself. There must be corroboration of each "crucial fact" (*factum probandum*). Crucial facts are "the elements which need to be established if the accused is to be found guilty of the crime in question" (*Smith* v *Lees* (1997), per the Lord Justice-General (Rodger) at 79). In other words, there must be corroboration of each element of the offence – including *mens rea*, where relevant – and of the accused's identity as the offender. So, for example, in *Lockwood* v *Walker* (1910) there was corroborated evidence that the accused had engaged in sexual activity with the complainer, but only one witness (the complainer herself) spoke to her age. Because the complainer's age was a crucial fact – the offence with which Lockwood was charged could only be committed where the girl was under the age of puberty – his conviction was quashed on appeal for lack of corroboration.

Facts which are not crucial, by contrast, may be proved by the evidence of one witness alone. In *Yates* v *HM Advocate* (1977), the accused was charged with rape, and it was alleged in the indictment that he had threatened the complainer with a knife. The only evidence that a knife had been used was that of the complainer herself. Nevertheless, the jury convicted him without deleting the allegation that a knife had been used. The court rejected his appeal, observing that the use of a knife was not a crucial element of the crime of rape. Provided that the essential elements of the crime had been proven by corroborated evidence, the jury were entitled to consider themselves satisfied that a knife had been used and find him guilty as libelled, despite there being no corroboration of that particular allegation.

What type of evidence can provide corroboration?

Corroborative evidence has been defined as "evidence which supports or confirms the direct evidence of a witness" (*Fox* v *HM Advocate* (1998), per the Lord Justice-General (Rodger) at 100). Although this definition is correct for most purposes, it must be remembered that there is no requirement for *any* direct evidence in order to secure a conviction, as a person may be convicted on indirect ("circumstantial") evidence alone (see, for example, *Little* v *HM Advocate* (1983)).

At one point, it was thought that, for evidence to be corroborative, it required to be "more consistent" with the incriminating evidence than with the account given by the accused (*Mackie* v *HM Advocate* (1994)). It was decided in *Fox* v *HM Advocate*, however, that there was no such requirement. The facts of *Fox* illustrate the difficulty: in that case, the complainer alleged that the accused had sexual intercourse with her while she was asleep (whereupon she woke up). The accused, by contrast, claimed that the intercourse had been consensual, but that the complainer had asked him to stop when she realised that he was not who she thought he was. The accused was charged with the crime of "clandestine injury". The direct evidence against him was that of the complainer herself and, for corroboration, the Crown relied on evidence that she had been seen in a distressed state shortly after the intercourse. The accused appealed against his conviction, arguing that the complainer's distress was no more consistent with her version of events than with his. The appeal court overruled *Mackie* and refused the appeal, holding that it was sufficient that the corroborative evidence supported the complainer's version of events.

It is possible, therefore, for evidence to be corroborative despite not being strongly incriminating. This is demonstrated by the way in which the courts have approached two particularly common problems: corroboration of identification and of confessions.

Identification

Although there must be two pieces of evidence tending to identify the accused as the perpetrator, "where one starts with an emphatic positive identification by one witness then very little else is required" (*Ralston v HM Advocate* (1987), per the Lord Justice-General (Emslie) at 472). Where, then, there is a clear identification, it suffices for the purposes of corroboration that a second witness has said that the accused resembles the perpetrator, or has given a description of the perpetrator that is consistent with the accused (see, for example, *Mair v HM Advocate* (1997)).

Confessions

Because a confession – as a statement against interest – is regarded as particularly strong evidence against an accused, it is often thought that the requisite corroboration need not be particularly strong. So, for example, when faced with the "clearest admission" of murder in *Hartley v HM Advocate* (1979), Lord Avonside remarked that "very little corroboration is required". In the later case of *Meredith v Lees* (1992), however, the appeal court expressed caution about this language:

> "There is a risk that, by describing the requirement in minimal terms by using the words such as 'very little' and then elevating it into a rule, there will be a weakening of the principle that there must be a sufficient independent check of the confession to corroborate it." (per the Lord Justice-General (Hope) at 131)

What amounts to a "sufficient independent check" will vary according to the facts of the case.

It must be remembered, of course, that the presence of corroboration does not necessarily mean that the accused should be convicted. Even if there is corroboration, the jury (or judge, in summary procedure) may conclude that the prosecution case has not been proven beyond reasonable doubt. Corroboration is a necessary condition for a conviction, but not a sufficient one.

Special means of providing corroboration

There are a number of "special cases" where particular rules about corroboration have been developed by the courts. These are sometimes described as "exceptions" to the corroboration requirement, but that is fundamentally incorrect – instead, they represent special means of providing corroboration.

Special knowledge confessions

In *Manuel* v *HM Advocate* (1958), the accused made a confession to murder which included a claim that the victim's body and a shoe belonging to her were buried in two different places in a field. He subsequently went to the field with police officers and identified certain places where digging revealed that the victim and her shoe were indeed buried. It was held that the finding of the body and the shoe could amount to corroboration of his confession.

Although the court in *Manuel* referred to Manuel's "actings" of assisting with subsequent discovery of evidence as corroboration, it is now clear that such actions are not necessary. What is important is that the confession demonstrates "special knowledge", even if this is already known to the police. In *Wilson* v *McAughey* (1982), the accused described the way in which a mechanical digger had been damaged, stolen and driven into a river. It was held that his confession could be corroborated by the state in which the digger had been found by the police, which was consistent with the facts disclosed in his confession.

Where special knowledge is demonstrated, the confession is sometimes described as "self-corroborating", although the corroborating evidence is independent evidence of the facts said to amount to special knowledge – facts which the accused could not have known without participation in or at least presence at the scene of the crime (but see *Wilson* v *HM Advocate* (1987), where it was held not to be fatal that the "special knowledge" demonstrated by the accused persons was also in the public domain – that was a matter to be considered by the jury in weighing the evidence).

Where the prosecution wishes to rely on a special knowledge confession to establish a sufficiency of evidence, it is necessary that the making of the confession itself is corroborated: that is, two persons must give evidence of the confession (*Low* v *HM Advocate* (1994)).

Distress as corroboration

In sexual offences, the only witness to the event – other than the accused – will often be the complainer. In such cases, the courts have consistently held (in a line of cases dating from *Yates* v *HM Advocate* (1977)) that evidence that the complainer was seen in a state of distress shortly after the alleged offence can serve as evidence corroborative of her account.

The logic of this approach is that the complainer's distressed state is an objective fact which is distinct from her own testimony: it is "evidence separate from and independent of that of the [complainer]" (*Smith* v *Lees* (1997), per Lord McCluskey at 108).

Evidence of distress cannot serve as corroboration of every crucial fact. In *Smith* v *Lees* (1997), the accused was alleged to have committed lewd, indecent and libidinous practices in a tent with a 13-year-old girl, who had been seen coming out of the tent with a tear in her eye (which was accepted as evidence of distress). The appeal court held that evidence of her distress was only evidence that something distressing had happened in the tent, but not of what actual acts had taken place. Accordingly, there was insufficient evidence to convict the accused.

However, in cases where the actual acts are not disputed – for example, where an accused is charged with rape and admits sexual intercourse but claims that the victim consented – evidence of distress can serve as corroboration of the victim's lack of consent. (The doctrine is not strictly limited to proving the absence of consent in sexual offences, although in practice this is its primary function.)

It must be shown that the distress is related to the incident, and so a lapse of time between the initial incident and the distress being observed may mean that it is incapable of being regarded as corroborative. See, for example, *McCrann* v *HM Advocate* (2003), where a rape was alleged to have been committed one evening but the complainer was not observed in a distressed state until 1 pm the next day (having appeared "happy and relaxed" up until then). It was held that there was insufficient evidence to relate her distress to the alleged rape.

If evidence of distress is regarded as independent of the distressed person's own testimony, it should follow that other emotional reactions may be of similar evidential value in appropriate cases. That logic was applied in *Fulton* v *HM Advocate* (2000), where F was charged with being in possession of a gun. The evidence against him consisted of his landlord's evidence that the gun was not his (and that he had previously seen it in F's possession outside the flat), together with the evidence of a police officer that the landlord had appeared "visibly shocked" when the gun had been discovered during a search. A majority of the appeal court held that evidence of the landlord's distress could corroborate his evidence, allowing the jury to infer that the gun was F's. (The conclusion was, however, only possible, as a matter of logic, if it had been established that the gun had to be either F's or the landlord's, and it was held in a subsequent appeal that this had not been established: *Fulton* v *HM Advocate* (2005)).

The Moorov *doctrine*

Another means of addressing the practical problem of the lack of witnesses to sexual offences is found in the *Moorov* doctrine, which is named after the case of *Moorov* v *HM Advocate* (1930). In that case, the accused, who ran a draper's shop, was charged with a series of assaults and indecent assaults on various female employees over a period of some years. In respect of many of the charges, the only direct evidence against him was that of the employee herself. The appeal court held that the evidence of the individual employees could corroborate other similar allegations, provided that the evidence was such as to indicate that the various incidents were connected: in the words of Lord Justice-General Clyde (at 73), "as subordinates in some particular and ascertained unity of intent, project, campaign, or adventure".

Although the doctrine is most important in respect of sexual offences, it is not limited to such cases. It has been applied, for example, to a series of attempts to bribe professional footballers (*McCudden* v *HM Advocate* (1952)) and a series of apparently motiveless assaults with a razor (*HM Advocate* v *McQuade* (1951)).

In order for the doctrine to apply, the crimes must be "so inter-related by character, circumstances and time ... as to justify an inference that they are instances of a course of criminal conduct systematically pursued by the accused person" (*Ogg* v *HM Advocate* (1938), per the Lord Justice-Clerk (Aitchison) at 157). There must also be evidence in respect of each crime identifying the accused as the offender in each case, although this need not be eyewitness evidence (*Lindsay* v *HM Advocate* (1994)).

The relationship of "character and circumstance" (the two are normally considered together) does not require that the offences be identical. What matters is that they are sufficiently factually connected. As Lord Aitchison pointed out in *Ogg* (at 157–158), "[f]orgery of a will may be relevant to a charge of murder, or the theft of a motor car to a charge of bank robbery". So, for example, it was held in *Carpenter* v *Hamilton* (1994) that a charge of breach of the peace and another of indecent exposure were sufficiently closely linked. They had occurred in the same location at around the same time of day, and the breach of the peace charge involved elements of indecency (making a suggestive noise and then following the complainer from behind some bushes).

The necessary relationship in time will depend on the nature of the offence: "[a] man whose course of conduct is to buy houses, insure them, and burn them down, or to acquire ships, insure them, and scuttle them, or to purport to marry women, defraud and desert them, cannot repeat the offence every month, or even perhaps every six months" (*Moorov*, per

Lord Sands at 89). Furthermore, the more similar the crimes, the greater the latitude in time that will be allowed. The appeal court has allowed a gap of as long as 3 years where the offences were particularly similar (*Turner* v *Scott* (1995)) and has suggested that a gap of even 4 years may not prevent *Moorov* applying (*Stewart* v *HM Advocate* (2007)). Normally, however, the court has been unwilling to apply *Moorov* in cases involving gaps of 3½ years or more (*Russell* v *HM Advocate* (1990); *Bargon* v *HM Advocate* (1997)), while stressing that no hard and fast rule will be laid down, and the applicability of the *Moorov* doctrine depends on the facts of each case.

Howden v HM Advocate

It was noted earlier that the *Moorov* doctrine requires evidence identifying the accused in respect of each charge. The difficulty with this restriction was demonstrated in *Howden* v *HM Advocate* (1994), where the accused was charged with attempting to rob both a building society and a bank. There were three eyewitnesses identifying him as the person who attempted to rob the building society, but none who identified him in respect of the bank. The appeal court held that, if the jury were satisfied beyond reasonable doubt that both offences had been committed by the same person, they could convict H of both offences despite the lack of identification in respect of one charge. It was denied that this was an application of the *Moorov* doctrine, but the principle involved is a similar one.

    Howden was applied in the subsequent case of *Townsley* v *Lees* (1996), and its correctness was later upheld in *Gillan* v *HM Advocate* (2002). The *Howden* principle does not do away with the need for corroboration of the accused's identity: in both cases there was more than one witness identifying the accused. Given that *Moorov* does not require direct eyewitness identification in respect of each charge, but allows the identification to be by inference, it might be argued that *Howden* is simply an application of the *Moorov* principle rather than a separate doctrine. The approach of the courts thus far, however, has been to regard it as a separate rule.

Similar fact evidence

It seems that the *Moorov* doctrine can only be applied where the accused is tried for all the relevant offences simultaneously (*Walsh* v *HM Advocate* (1961)). However, it might be that this cannot be done, perhaps – for example – because some of the offences took place too long ago to be prosecuted, have already been prosecuted, or took place outwith the jurisdiction of the court. In such cases, can the evidence of these offences be used as corroboration? The position in Scots law is undeveloped and uncertain. In the case of *HM Advocate* v *Joseph* (1929), the prosecution was permitted to lead evidence of a fraud committed in Belgium in support of allegations of a series of frauds committed in Scotland. Although the evidence appears not to have been essential for the purposes of corroboration, the fact that it was admissible in support of the allegations against J suggests that it should have been permissible to rely on it in order to satisfy the corroboration requirement if necessary.

The decision in *Joseph* reflects principles of "similar fact evidence", a doctrine rather broader than (but potentially encompassing) *Moorov*. In England, the courts have taken this principle so far as to allow evidence of alleged rapes – of which the defendant had previously been acquitted – to be led in support of a fresh prosecution for rape (*R* v *Z* (2000)). There are strong arguments for the Scottish courts recognising a single doctrine of similar fact evidence, which would incorporate both *Moorov* and *Howden*. This has not yet happened (see P Duff, "Towards a unified theory of 'similar facts evidence' in Scots law" 2002 JR 143), but this area of law was under review by the Scottish Law Commission at the time of writing, with a report due to be published in early 2012.

Reform of the law of corroboration

In late 2010, the Scottish Government asked Lord Carloway, a senior judge, to review elements of Scottish criminal law and practice in the light of the decision in *Cadder* v *HM Advocate* (2010, discussed in Chapter 7). *The Carloway Review: Report and Recommendations* was published in late 2011. In his report, Lord Carloway attacked corroboration as "an archaic rule that has no place in a modern legal system" (para 7.2.55) and recommended that it be abolished. Lord Carloway's view is that the requirement of proof beyond reasonable doubt provides sufficient protection for the accused, and that the corroboration requirement results in the system being "skewed by prioritising quantity over quality [of evidence]" (para 7.2.44). This proved the most immediately controversial aspect of the report, and the Scottish Government is expected to consult further on this issue before reaching a final decision on any possible legislation.

Corroboration in civil cases

Historically, the corroboration requirement applied in civil cases in the same way as criminal ones. However, it has now been abolished in its entirety (Civil Evidence (Scotland) Act 1988, s 1) and so a civil case may be proved on the evidence of one witness alone. There is now nothing to bar a case being proved on the evidence of the pursuer alone.

In a small category of cases, however – actions for declarator of marriage, nullity of marriage, divorce or separation (and analogous actions in respect of civil partnerships) – the evidence in support of the pursuer's case must include evidence from someone who is not one of the parties (or alleged parties) to the marriage or civil partnership (Civil Evidence (Scotland) Act 1988, s 8, as amended). This is not a corroboration requirement, as a person meeting this requirement can be the *only* witness.

It was noted earlier (Chapter 2) that there were some types of civil case which had to be proven to the standard of "beyond reasonable doubt" – the standard which applies in criminal proceedings – rather than the normal civil standard of the "balance of probabilities". Although the higher standard of proof applies to such cases, the corroboration requirement generally does not (*Byrne* v *Ross* (1992)).

Essential Facts

- No one can be convicted of a criminal offence unless the prosecution case is proved by corroborated evidence. The rule is subject to only minor statutory exceptions.

- Every "crucial fact" – that is, every element of the criminal offence, and the accused's identity as the offender – must be corroborated.

- Other facts need not be proved by corroborated evidence.

- Evidence is corroborative if it "supports or confirms" incriminating evidence.

- A confession may be corroborated by "special knowledge" where it demonstrates knowledge of facts of which the accused could not have been aware had he not been present at the scene of the crime.

- In sexual offences, the fact that the complainer was witnessed in a distressed state shortly after the event may serve to corroborate her claim that she did not consent to sexual activity.

- Where an accused is charged with a number of offences "inter-related by character, circumstance and time", the evidence led to prove one offence may corroborate the allegation that the accused has committed another of those offences. This is known as the *Moorov* doctrine.

- The requirement of corroboration has been abolished in respect of civil cases.

Essential Cases

Fox v HM Advocate (1998): evidence is corroborative if it "supports or confirms" other evidence.

HM Advocate v Joseph (1929): it was permissible to lead evidence of a fraud committed in Belgium in support of allegations of a (related) series of frauds committed in Scotland.

Howden v HM Advocate (1994): where it is proved that the same person must have committed two (or more) different offences, but there is no evidence identifying the accused in respect of one of the charges, it is nevertheless competent to convict the accused of all the charges, provided that there are still overall two sources of evidence in respect of each crucial fact, including identification.

Meredith v Lees (1992): evidence corroborating a confession must provide a "sufficient independent check" on the confession.

Moorov v HM Advocate (1930): where an accused is charged with a series of offences so inter-related in character, circumstances and time so as to suggest that they are part of a single course of criminal conduct, evidence in respect of one offence can corroborate evidence in respect of another offence. There must be evidence identifying the accused in respect of each charge.

Smith v Lees (1997): evidence of distress on the part of the complainer is evidence that "something distressing" has taken place, and so can corroborate the complainer's evidence that she did not consent to what happened. It cannot, however, corroborate the complainer's evidence as to the type of act which was involved.

5 THE RULE AGAINST HEARSAY

This chapter is concerned with the rule against hearsay – at its simplest, a rule which prevents a witness from giving evidence of what another person has said. As will be seen, however, the definition of "hearsay" is slightly more complex than that. Furthermore, understanding the rule against hearsay is, in practice, as much a question of understanding the multitude of exceptions to the rule as understanding the rule itself.

The rule against hearsay was abolished in relation to civil cases in 1988. Accordingly, this chapter is concerned largely with the criminal law only, but the position in civil cases is set out at the end of this chapter (pp 41–42).

Why exclude hearsay?

There are two main justifications for excluding hearsay evidence:

- It is seen as *inherently unreliable*. In particular, hearsay evidence is not subject to the test of cross-examination, and the judge or jury is unable to see and evaluate the demeanour of the witness. On this argument, the evidence is of limited value and may well mislead.

- It is *not the best evidence available*. On this argument, hearsay evidence should be excluded in favour of evidence from the original statement maker. Allowing hearsay evidence might lead to unnecessary duplication of testimony and unduly prolong the course of a trial or proof.

It will readily be seen that these two arguments have different consequences. For example, if the maker of the original statement were dead or otherwise unable to give evidence, a "best evidence" approach could be used to justify admitting hearsay evidence of his statement. An "inherent unreliability" approach, however, might lead to the conclusion that the hearsay evidence should remain inadmissible.

The "inherent unreliability" approach, however, would allow for exceptions to the hearsay rule where the hearsay evidence was seen as being particularly reliable – which is one argument for admitting evidence of confessions by an accused person, on the basis that people are (supposedly) highly unlikely to confess to acts they have not carried out.

At common law, in admitting of exceptions to the hearsay rule, Scots law appears to have afforded more weight to arguments based on reliability than a "best evidence" approach. However, the rule against hearsay has recently been reformed by statute – ss 259–260 of the Criminal Procedure (Scotland) Act 1995 – which is more closely modelled on "best evidence" principles. All of this can be seen through an examination of the exceptions to the rule against hearsay, which form the best part of this chapter, but it is first necessary to consider exactly what "hearsay" evidence is.

Defining hearsay

A number of different definitions – not always consistent – of hearsay may be found in the literature. The Scottish courts have accepted the following definition: "an assertion other than one made by a person while giving oral evidence in the proceedings is inadmissible *as evidence of any fact asserted*" (*Morrison* v *HM Advocate* (1990), per the Lord Justice-Clerk (Ross) at 312).

The rule against hearsay, therefore, prevents evidence of a statement made outside court being led in order to prove the truth of its contents. It does *not*, however, prevent such evidence being led if the party seeks only to prove that the statement was made, regardless of its truth. The distinction is illustrated by the decision of the Privy Council in *Subramaniam* v *Public Prosecutor* (1956), where S pled the defence of duress (the equivalent of the Scottish plea of coercion) and sought to give evidence of threats he claimed had been made against him by terrorists. The trial judge ruled that this was inadmissible hearsay, but the Privy Council held that this was wrong: for the purposes of S's defence, what mattered was whether the threats were made, not whether they were true. The Privy Council explained (at 970):

> "Evidence of a statement made to a witness by a person who is not himself called as a witness may or may not be hearsay. It is hearsay and inadmissible when the object of the evidence is to establish the truth of what is contained in the statement. It is not hearsay and is admissible when it is proposed to establish by the evidence, not the truth of the statement, but the fact that it is made."

Confusingly, evidence such as that in *Subramaniam* is referred to by some writers as "primary hearsay". Where this terminology is used, it is meant to indicate that "primary hearsay" is admissible: where the party seeks to rely on the statement as proof of its contents, it is "secondary hearsay", and is inadmissible.

Implied assertions

The hearsay rule strikes only against using evidence of another person's statement "as evidence of any fact or opinion asserted" (*Morrison*, above). On the basis of that definition, the Scottish Law Commission has suggested that a statement is inadmissible hearsay only when a party seeks to use it as evidence of a fact which the person making it *intended* to assert – as opposed to a fact which is implicit in the statement. (See *Evidence: Report on Hearsay Evidence in Criminal Proceedings* (Scot Law Com No 149, 1995), para 5.13.)

The distinction is illustrated by the case of *McLaren* v *Macleod* (1913), where Mrs McLaren was charged with brothel-keeping, and the prosecution led evidence from two policemen who had overheard two women in the premises complaining about M having introduced "short time" to the house. The court held that this evidence was admissible. The logic of admitting it seems to be that the character of the premises as a brothel is something which could be inferred from the nature of the conversation (an "implied assertion"), rather than a claim which the overheard women intended to make in their statements.

Implied assertions caused some difficulty in English law until recently, with the House of Lords holding by a majority that evidence that a number of persons had requested to buy drugs from the defendant was inadmissible hearsay and could not be used to prove that he was dealing in drugs (*R* v *Kearley* (1992)). Although the Scottish courts suggested shortly afterwards that this approach would not be followed in Scotland (*Lord Advocate's Reference (No 1 of 1992)* (1992), per the Lord Justice-General (Hope) at 189), more recent decisions of the Scottish courts seem to have assumed that such evidence is inadmissible (*Ogilvie* v *HM Advocate* (1999); *Hamill* v *HM Advocate* (1999)), and so the position is now unclear. In English law, *Kearley* is no longer good law and such evidence is admissible (see s 115(3) of the Criminal Justice Act 2003, which does not apply to Scotland).

De recenti *statements*

In some circumstances, it may be possible to lead evidence of a statement made by the alleged victim of a sexual assault shortly after the event, for the purpose of bolstering their credibility by showing that their version of events has been consistent from the outset. In such cases, the evidence is not struck at by the hearsay rule because it is not led to prove the truth of the statement itself. Such a statement is relevant only where the witness's credibility is in issue, and so can normally be used only where the victim himself or herself gives evidence.

This is referred to as evidence of a *de recenti* statement. Although it has been said that such evidence "may theoretically be admissible in any case" (*Walkers on Evidence* (3rd edn, 2009), para 8.3.1) it appears, in practice, to be restricted to statements made by the victim of a sexual assault (*Morton v HM Advocate* (1938)).

In the unusual case of *Ahmed* v *HM Advocate* (2010), it was held that a *de recenti* statement by the complainer that she had been raped could be admitted in evidence even though the complainer denied that she had made the statement. The court observed (at para 18) that "a denial that she made the statement may, just as testimony that she has no recollection of so doing, be for one or more of a number of reasons which are wholly consistent with the truth and accuracy of her testimony about the attack".

Admitting prior statements: exceptions to the rule against hearsay

In some circumstances, hearsay evidence may be admissible in a criminal trial. Any examination of the law of hearsay is largely a study of these exceptions, and most of this chapter is a description of them.

It should be noted, however, that even where a prior statement of an individual is admissible as an exception to the hearsay rule, this excludes what are termed "precognitions". A precognition is a statement taken from a witness which is not in the witness's own words, but has been "filtered through the mind of another". The reasons for this rule were explained in *Kerr* v *HM Advocate* (1958), where the Lord Justice-Clerk (Thomson) said (at 19):

> "one reason why reference to precognition is frowned on, is that in a precognition you cannot be sure that you are getting what the potential witness has to say in a pure and undefiled form. It is filtered through the mind of another, whose job it is to put what he thinks the witness means into a form suitable for use in judicial proceedings. This process tends to colour the result. Precognosers as a rule appear to be gifted with a measure of optimism which no amount of disillusionment can damp".

In the same case, the Lord Justice-Clerk said (at 18) that "[w]hat amounts to a precognition is a question of some considerable difficulty", and depends largely on the extent to which the statement is in the victim's own words or has been written by another person in response to questioning. It is certainly not the case that any statement taken by the police will be held to be a precognition. For example, in *Irving* v *HM Advocate* (1978) a rape victim's statement to the police was held not to be a precognition, probably because there had been very little questioning of the now-deceased complainer except for some points of clarification. In *Highland Venison Marketing Ltd* v *Allwild GmbH* (1992), Lord Cullen observed that the fact that a witness had prepared a revised version of a precognition and had it retyped meant that there was a strong case for saying that it had ceased to be a precognition, but in the circumstances of that case it was unnecessary for him to decide that point.

Whether or not a statement is a precognition is a question of law for the judge (*HM Advocate* v *McSween* (2007)).

Common law exceptions to the rule against hearsay

The principal common law exceptions to the rule against hearsay are set out below. In principle, this is not a closed list and it is open to the courts to create new exceptions (*Perrie* v *HM Advocate* (1991)). However, since *Perrie*, Parliament has passed legislation expanding the availability of exceptions to the hearsay rule (see below, pp 39–40), and so the courts are likely to be reluctant to engage in further judicial reform of the rule.

1. Statements forming part of the res gestae

Statements which form part of the *res gestae* are admissible as an exception to the rule against hearsay. The exact scope of this rule can be difficult to determine: in *Ratten* v *R* (1972), Lord Wilberforce remarked (at 388) that *res gestae*, "like many Latin phrases, is often used to cover situations insufficiently analysed in clear English terms". Wilkinson defines *res gestae* as "the whole circumstances immediately and directly connected with an occurrence which is part of the facts in issue" (*The Scottish Law of Evidence* (1986), p 39). In *Ratten*, it was suggested that the rationale for admitting such statements is that the circumstances in which they were made are "of involvement or pressure as to exclude the possibility of concoction or distortion" (per Lord Wilberforce at 391).

To similar effect, in *Teper* v *R* (1952), Lord Normand said (at 487) that "it is essential that the words sought to be proved by hearsay should be, if not absolutely contemporaneous with the action or event, at least so closely associated with it, in time, place and circumstances, that they are part of the thing being done, and so an item or part of real evidence and not merely a reported statement".

Examples of statements which have been held to be admissible as part of the *res gestae* include the following:

- *HM Advocate* v *Murray* (1866): "the first statement or exclamation" made by a mentally incompetent girl arriving home after an alleged sexual assault.

- *O'Hara* v *Central SMT Co* (1941): evidence that, immediately after a bus had been involved in an accident, a pedestrian (who could not be traced) had admitted to running in front of the bus.

But, in *Cinci* v *HM Advocate* (2004), the Lord Justice-Clerk (Gill) suggested that *O'Hara* (and, by implication, some of the other cases) went too far. In that case, a victim had been heard to say "he raped me" while the accused was leaning over her immediately after sexual intercourse had taken place. Lord Gill said (at para 12): "If the words spoken, though closely related to the event, are not part of the event, they cannot be treated as part of the *res gestae* ... In *O'Hara* v *Central SMT Co*, in my view, the event had certainly ceased when the pedestrian made the admission". By contrast, Lord Gill said, if the woman had been heard to shout "stop it" while intercourse was taking place, evidence of that statement would have been admissible.

2. Death, incapacity and unavailability

At common law, hearsay evidence was admissible where the maker of the statement was dead, permanently insane or a prisoner of war (although the last of these exceptions might have applied to civil cases only). (See *HM Advocate* v *Monson* (1897), per the Lord Justice-Clerk (Macdonald) at 9–10.) In *McKie* v *Western Scottish Motor Traction Co* (1952), the Inner House reserved opinion on whether the same exception applied to a witness "disabled by illness" from giving evidence. The common law rules are now effectively superseded by statute, which provides for a wider exception to the rule against hearsay in such cases than that permitted at common law (see below, p 39).

3. Statements against interest

It is assumed that statements against interest (including confessions) are especially reliable, because persons are unlikely to make inaccurate statements to their own prejudice. Accordingly, these are admitted as an exception to the hearsay rule. (Evidence of a statement against interest may, however, be excluded where it was unfairly obtained, a matter which is dealt with in Chapter 7.)

The statement cannot be made by a third party. A useful example is provided by the case of *Jackson* v *Glasgow Corporation* (1956) (decided when the rule against hearsay still applied in civil cases), where a woman brought an action in respect of a collision between a bus and a car driven by her husband. It was held that the defenders could not lead hearsay evidence that her husband had admitted he was at fault in the accident. However, where a statement was made by a third party in the presence of the accused, the accused's *reaction* to it may be admissible evidence: and so, for example, it was held in *Buchan* v *HM Advocate* (1995) that it was competent to prove that A had said "It was'nae me. It was Jamie done it" in front of Jamie in order to explain the significance of Jamie's reaction to this claim. The statement was not *in itself* evidence against Jamie, however. Whether a jury will feel able to apply such fine distinctions is a matter for speculation.

There is an exception to the general rule where it is proved that two or more accused were acting in concert. In such a case, the evidence of a statement against interest by one accused is evidence against all those party to the common criminal purpose (see, eg, *Hamill* v *HM Advocate* (1999)).

Where a director of a company made a statement against the interests of the company, this was held to be admissible against the company in a criminal prosecution (*Industrial Distributions (Central Scotland) Ltd* v *Quinn* (1984)).

Problems have occasionally arisen in respect of what are termed "mixed statements", which are partially incriminatory and partially exculpatory – for example, where the accused admits being at the scene of the crime (incriminatory) but claims that he saw someone else commit the offence (exculpatory) (as in *McIntosh* v *HM Advocate* (2003)). In such a case, if the prosecution leads evidence of the incriminating aspects of the statement, the defence is entitled to lead evidence of, and rely on, the exculpatory elements. This is an exception to the normal rule, as the appeal court explained in *McCutcheon* v *HM Advocate* (2002) (a decision of nine judges which is the leading case on the subject). The Lord Justice-General (Cullen) said (at para 16):

> "The main rules which apply are as follows: (i) It is a general rule that hearsay, that is evidence of what another person has said, is not admissible as evidence of the truth of what was said. (ii) Thus evidence of what an accused has been heard to say is, in general, not admissible in his exculpation, and accordingly the defence are not entitled to rely on it for this purpose. Such evidence can be relied on by the defence only for the purpose of proving that the statement was made, or of showing his attitude or reaction at the time when it was made, as part of the general picture which the jury have to consider. (iii) There is, however, an exception where the Crown have led evidence of a statement, part of which is capable of incriminating the accused. The defence are entitled to elicit and rely upon any part of that statement as qualifying, explaining or excusing the admission against interest."

4. *Evidence of prior identification or other statements*

In *Muldoon* v *Herron* (1970), two eyewitnesses to a crime gave evidence that, shortly after the offence, they had pointed out several of the persons involved to the police. They could not, however, identify those persons in court (and one gave evidence – not believed by the sheriff – that the three accused were not among the persons she had pointed out). Two police officers gave evidence that the three accused were among the persons who the eyewitnesses had pointed out.

On appeal, a Full Bench held that the sheriff had been right to admit the evidence of the police officers, although the court argued this was not hearsay – it was "direct and primary" evidence of who had been identified shortly after the offence.

In the later case of *Jamieson* v *HM Advocate (No 2)* (1994), the appeal court reaffirmed the validity of the *Muldoon* principle, and clarified its scope. According to the Lord Justice-General (Hope) (at 258):

> "the principle upon which the evidence of identification was held to be admissible in that case [*Muldoon*] is of wider application and is not confined to identification evidence ... if [a witness] is unable to recollect what he said to the police when he comes to give evidence, the gap in his recollection can be filled by what the police said he said to them at the time. This evidence, when taken with the witness's own evidence that he made a true statement at the time to the police, is held to be admissible because there are two primary sources of evidence. One is the evidence of the police officers as to who was in fact identified and the other is the witness's own evidence that he identified the culprit to the police ... neither of these facts proves identity, but both are elements in the structure of evidence from which identification may be held proved."

This suggests, therefore, that if the witness *denies* having made a true identification (or other statement) to the police, the police evidence would be inadmissible (but compare the earlier case of *Smith* v *HM Advocate* (1986), where the appeal court held that it was permissible for such evidence to go to the jury).

It will be noted that both the *Jamieson* and *Muldoon* courts deny that this creates an exception to the rule against hearsay (as have the English courts, although not in the same way: see *R* v *McCay* (1990), which relies on the existing *res gestae* exception). That has been doubted, and in a case decided between *Jamieson* and *Muldoon* the appeal court said that it *did* regard *Muldoon* as an exception to the rule against hearsay (*Frew* v *Jessop* (1990)). The debate may not matter very much as long as the rule's scope is clear.

Shortly after *Jamieson*, legislation was passed providing that a witness might "adopt" a prior statement when giving oral evidence. The relevant provision is now s 260 of the Criminal Procedure (Scotland) Act 1995, which provides that a prior statement – assuming its content is such that the witness could competently give direct oral evidence as to its subject-matter – may be admissible if:

(a) the statement is contained in a document;

(b) the witness, in the course of giving evidence, indicates that the statement was made by him and that he adopts it as his evidence; and

(c) at the time the statement was made, the person who made it would have been a competent witness in the proceedings.

In *Hughes* v *HM Advocate* (2009), the appeal court suggested that the rule in *Jamieson* was separate from that in s 260 and that either could be relied on to make use of a prior statement. If correct (which is doubtful), this would render s 260 largely redundant, and it is unfortunate that the *Hughes* court did not refer to the Scottish Law Commission report which led to that provision, which makes it clear that its aim was to embody the *ratio* of *Jamieson* in statute (*Evidence: Report on Hearsay Evidence in Criminal Proceedings* (Scot Law Com No 149, 1995), paras 7.8 and 7.43).

Statutory exceptions to the rule against hearsay

In addition to the common law exceptions noted above, and s 260 of the Criminal Procedure (Scotland) Act 1995, s 259 of that same Act enacts further exceptions to the rule against hearsay. As set out in s 259(2), these are that the person who made the original statement:

"(a) is dead or is, by reason of his bodily or mental condition, unfit or unable to give evidence in any competent manner;

(b) is named and otherwise sufficiently identified, but is outwith the United Kingdom and it is not reasonably practicable to secure his attendance at the trial or to obtain his evidence in any other competent manner;

(c) is named and otherwise sufficiently identified, but cannot be found and all reasonable steps which, in the circumstances, could have been taken to find him have been so taken;

(d) having been authorised to do so by virtue of a ruling of the court in the proceedings that he is entitled to refuse to give evidence in connection with the subject matter of the statement on the grounds that such evidence might incriminate him, refuses to give such evidence; or

(e) is called as a witness and either –

    (i) refuses to take the oath or affirmation; or

    (ii) having been sworn as a witness and directed by the judge to give evidence in connection with the subject matter of the statement refuses to do so, and in the application of this paragraph to a child, the reference to a witness refusing to take the oath or affirmation or, as the case may be, to having been sworn shall be construed as a reference to a child who has refused to accept an admonition to tell the truth or, having been so admonished, refuses to give evidence as mentioned above."

Subsections (a)–(c) expand and rationalise the common law rules relating to the death or unavailability of a witness. Subsections (d) and (e) effectively overrule the earlier decisions in *Perrie* v *HM Advocate* (1991) and *McLay* v *HM Advocate* (1994), where it was held that an accused could not, in his defence, lead hearsay evidence of a confession by a third party who refused to give evidence. If the third party did give evidence, then the hearsay evidence could be put to him as a prior inconsistent statement under s 263(4) of the 1995 Act (see p 77 below). In such a case, the prior statement would, strictly speaking, be evidence going only to the witness's credibility, rather than evidence of the truth of its contents, but it would nevertheless be brought out in court.

In *MacDonald* v *HM Advocate* (1999), the court emphasised that the requirements of subsection (e) are strict: it deals with a refusal to give evidence, rather than an inability or difficulty. Accordingly, it could not be used where a child broke down in the witness box and was unable to answer questions, in the absence of a specific direction from the judge to answer with which direction she had refused to comply.

In order for hearsay to be admitted under any of these exceptions, the judge must, under s 259(1), be satisfied:

"(a) that the person who made the statement will not give evidence in the proceedings of such matter for any of the [reasons specified in s 259(2)];

(b) that evidence of the matter would be admissible in the proceedings if that person gave direct oral evidence of it;

(c) that the person who made the statement would have been, at the time the statement was made, a competent witness in such proceedings; and

(d) that there is evidence which would entitle a jury properly directed, or in summary proceedings would entitle the judge, to find that the statement was made and that either –

    (i) it is contained in a document; or

    (ii) a person who gave oral evidence in the proceedings as to the statement has direct personal knowledge of the making of the statement."

Hearsay and the European Convention on Human Rights

The admission of hearsay evidence raises a potential conflict with Art 6 of the European Convention on Human Rights (the right to a fair trial), particularly Art 6(3)(d) which refers to the minimum right of an accused person "to examine or have examined witnesses against him". However, the European Court and Commission have consistently held that – where it is not possible to examine the maker of the original statement directly – the use of hearsay evidence will not violate the ECHR "provided that the rights of the defence have been respected" (*Ferrantelli and Santangelo* v *Italy* (1997) at para 51).

In one case, the High Court held that the use of hearsay evidence against an accused did violate his right under Art 6 due to the lack of any opportunity to cross-examine the statement maker about certain issues (*N* v *HM Advocate* (2003)). That case is probably best regarded as wholly exceptional, and there are a number of other cases where the Scottish courts have rejected Art 6 challenges to the use of hearsay evidence (see, eg, *McKenna* v *HM Advocate* (2003) and *Daly* v *HM Advocate* (2003), which were decided alongside *N*). More recently, the European Court of Human Rights has explained that a requirement of corroboration may operate as a safeguard against the use of hearsay evidence being a violation of Art 6 (*Al-Khawaja and Tahery* v *United Kingdom* (2012)).

Hearsay in civil cases

The rule against hearsay in civil cases was abolished by the Civil Evidence (Scotland) Act 1988, s 2(1) of which provides:

> "In any civil proceedings –
> (a) evidence shall not be excluded solely on the ground that it is hearsay;
> (b) a statement made by a person otherwise than in the course of the proof shall be admissible as evidence of any matter contained in the statement of which direct oral evidence by that person would be admissible; and
> (c) the court, or as the case may be the jury, if satisfied that any fact has been established by evidence in those proceedings, shall be entitled to find that fact proved by the evidence notwithstanding that the evidence is hearsay."

According to s 9 of the 1988 Act, the term "statement" "does not include a statement in a precognition". (As to what is meant by a "precognition", see p 34 above.) Accordingly, the view has been taken that precognitions remain inadmissible in civil proceedings (*McAvoy* v *Glasgow District Council* (1993), but compare *Highland Venison Marketing Ltd* v *Allwild GmbH* (1992), where Lord Cullen suggested, *obiter*, that precognitions were now admissible in civil proceedings as a result of the 1988 Act). It is permissible, however, for a precognoser to give oral hearsay evidence of what the third party said to them (see, for example, *Anderson* v *Jas B Fraser & Co Ltd* (1992)).

The wording of s 2 gave rise for some time to problems in respect of hearsay statements made by children. Because s 2(1)(b) requires that the hearsay statement be one "of which direct oral evidence by [the maker] would be admissible", it was thought that the hearsay evidence could only be used if it were established first that the child were a competent witness, which would probably require the child to be examined in court to establish competency (something which was required for children giving evidence prior to s 24 of the Vulnerable Witnesses (Scotland) Act 2004, which abolished the competency test).

This created two difficulties – first, that it partially negated a common reason for using hearsay evidence, to avoid a child having to go into the witness box, and secondly, that it was not clear at what date competency was to be assessed – was it at the date the statement was made, or at the date of the proof? (See, among other cases, *F* v *Kennedy (No 1)* (1992); *L* v *L* (1996).)

The problem has now been resolved by a Full Bench decision in *MT* v *DT* (2001), where it was held that s 2 does not require a competency test. According to the court, s 2(1)(b) ensures simply that hearsay evidence is subject to the same rules of competency and relevancy as direct oral evidence. It does not require the competency of the maker of the original statement to be assessed before the hearsay evidence is led.

Essential Facts

The rule against hearsay

- The rule against hearsay prevents evidence of a statement made by another person being led as proof of any fact asserted in that statement.

- The rule does not prevent evidence of a statement made by another person being led simply as evidence of the fact that it was made.

- The rule may not prevent evidence of such a statement being led as evidence of a fact *implied* in that statement, but the position is unclear.

- Evidence of a statement made by the alleged victim of a sexual assault shortly after the event may be admissible as evidence that the victim is a credible witness (in that it shows their story has been consistent), but it is not evidence of the truth of its contents.
- The rule against hearsay has been abolished in respect of civil cases.

Exceptions to the rule against hearsay

- Statements made in "precognitions" – a statement which is not in the witness's own words, but "filtered through the mind of another" – are never admissible, even where an exception to the hearsay rule applies.
- At common law, the following exceptions to the rule against hearsay are recognised:
  - Statements forming part of the *res gestae* – that is, statements made during the event itself or (perhaps) in closely connected circumstances.
  - Statements made by a person who is now dead or permanently insane.
  - Statements against interest (such as confessions). Where a statement is "mixed" – partly inculpatory and partly exculpatory – the prosecution may lead evidence of the incriminatory elements, but the defence may then rely on the exculpatory elements.
  - Statements made to the police which are then "adopted" by a witness when giving evidence in court.
- Further exceptions are now recognised by statute (s 259 of the Criminal Procedure (Scotland) Act 1995) (set out at pp 39–40 above).

Essential Cases

Cinci v HM Advocate (2004): a statement made during the incident itself is admissible as part of the *res gestae* exception to the rule against hearsay, but earlier cases where it was suggested that statements made shortly thereafter can also be admissible are open to doubt.

Jamieson v HM Advocate (No 2) (1994): a witness may, when giving evidence, "adopt" a prior statement made to the police.

Kerr v HM Advocate (1958): a precognition is a statement "filtered through the mind of another" and is not admissible even where an exception to the rule against hearsay applies.

McCutcheon v HM Advocate (2002): the leading case on "mixed statements", where it was held that the prosecution could rely on the incriminating aspects of such statements, but that the defence was then entitled to rely on the exculpatory aspects as "qualifying, explaining or excusing" the incriminatory ones.

Morrison v HM Advocate (1990): defines the rule against hearsay as "an assertion other than one made by a person while giving oral evidence in the proceedings is inadmissible *as evidence of any fact asserted*".

Subramaniam v Public Prosecutor (1956): evidence from a person accused of a crime that he had been coerced into committing it by threats from terrorists was admissible, as the evidence was led to show simply that the threats were made, not that they were true.

6 THE "BEST EVIDENCE" RULE

According to Dickson, "a party must adduce the best attainable evidence of the facts he means to prove" (*A Treatise on the Law of Evidence in Scotland* (3rd edn, 1887), para 195). Although it has been said that, in modern practice, "the best evidence rule is no longer a principle of general application" (Wilkinson, *The Scottish Law of Evidence* (1986), p 10), it continues to be of importance in the narrow context of real evidence – and, to a much lesser extent, in the case of documentary evidence.

Real evidence

The relevant principle is set out in *Macleod v Woodmuir Miners Welfare Society Social Club* (1961), per the Lord Justice-General (Clyde) at 9: "Primary evidence is not always essential, and secondary evidence is not necessarily incompetent. Secondary evidence is competent if it is not reasonably practicable and convenient to produce the primary evidence."

This principle was applied to exclude evidence in *McGowan v Belling & Co Ltd* (1983), a civil case based on an allegation that an electric heater was faulty. Two expert witnesses gave evidence based on their examination of a similar heater, but it could not be confirmed that the relevant parts were the same because the heater they had examined – although still available – was not produced in court. In those circumstances, Lord Cowie ruled that this heater, as the "best evidence of its type and condition", should have been lodged and therefore "an oral description of its condition in its absence was inadmissible and any expert evidence based on its alleged condition was also inadmissible".

However, *McGowan v Belling* may signal the high-water mark of the "best evidence" rule. In the criminal case of *McKellar v Normand* (1992), the appellant was charged with the reset of a bed and blanket, which were not produced in evidence. Her appeal against conviction was rejected on the basis that she had not been prejudiced by the failure to produce the items. The Lord Justice-General (Hope) stated (at 394–395):

> "It is good practice for items which are the subject of charges of this kind to be produced if it is convenient to do so or, failing production, for labels relating to the items to be produced in their place. But the question must always be, if an objection is taken as to the admissibility of the evidence, whether in the absence of the items or labels relating to them some injustice is likely to result to the accused."

That suggests that the question may now be one of prejudice alone. (It may be that *McGowan* still governs civil cases and that the rule applies more strictly in civil than criminal cases, but that would sit oddly with the general tendency to apply stricter rules of evidence in criminal cases. In any event, although Lord Cowie's reasoning in *McGowan* was not founded on prejudice, it is easy to see how the defenders in that case might have been prejudiced by the failure to produce the heater.) Even if secondary evidence is admissible, of course, the court may not feel able to give it the same weight as primary evidence.

Furthermore, even if it is impracticable to produce primary evidence, a failure to allow one party to examine the item in question may lead to prejudice. In *Anderson* v *Laverock* (1976), the court was satisfied that it was competent to lead secondary evidence of fish of which the accused was alleged to have been in possession unlawfully, as the fish were perishable and it was not reasonably practicable and convenient to retain them. However, the accused had not been notified that the evidence was to be disposed of and given an opportunity to examine it, something which was crucial because the physical appearance of the fish was crucial to the Crown case (as indicating the way in which they were caught) and Crown witnesses had been cross-examined at length about this. Accordingly, the appeal court held that the accused had been prejudiced by this lack of opportunity and his conviction had to be quashed.

Situations such as that in *Anderson* v *Laverock* are now governed by s 276 of the Criminal Procedure (Scotland) Act 1995, which provides as follows:

> "(1) Evidence as to the characteristics and composition of any biological material deriving from human beings or animals shall, in any criminal proceedings, be admissible notwithstanding that neither the material nor a sample of it is lodged as a production.
>
> (2) A party wishing to lead such evidence as is referred to in subsection (1) above shall, where neither the material nor a sample of it is lodged as a production, make the material or a sample of it available for inspection by the other party unless the material constitutes a hazard to health or has been destroyed in the process of analysis."

Documentary evidence

Civil cases

The "best evidence" rule applies to documentary as well as real evidence, and was applied in *Scottish & Universal Newspapers* v *Gherson's Trs* (1988) to exclude evidence of copy documents where the originals had been lost due to fault on the part of the pursuers (who wished to lead the copies in evidence). However, the rule is effectively relaxed by s 6 of the Civil Evidence (Scotland) Act 1988, which provides as follows:

"(1) For the purposes of any civil proceedings, a copy of a document, purporting to be authenticated by a person responsible for the making of the copy, shall, unless the court otherwise directs, be –

(a) deemed a true copy; and

(b) treated for evidential purposes as if it were the document itself.

(2) In subsection (1) above, 'copy' includes a transcript or reproduction."

If the copy is not authenticated, the "best evidence" rule continues to apply. It had been suggested that unauthenticated copies might still be admissible (although not given the same weight) given that the 1988 Act had also abolished the rule against hearsay in civil proceedings (see above, p 41). However, in *Japan Leasing (Europe) plc* v *Weir's Tr (No 2)* (1998), the Inner House held that, despite the abolition of the hearsay rule, the "best evidence" rule could still operate to bar the use of unauthenticated copy documents as evidence in civil proceedings.

Criminal cases

There are now similar (although not absolutely identical) statutory provisions to s 6 of the 1988 Act which apply to civil proceedings: Criminal Procedure (Scotland) Act 1995, s 279 and Sch 8, para 1.

In addition, paras 2 and 3 of Sch 8 contain specific provisions relating to business documents. These allow statements contained in such documents to be admissible as proof of their contents (and also allow for a statement to be made, and accepted in evidence, to the effect that business documents do "not contain a relevant statement as to a particular matter"). This goes further than simply allowing a copy document to be treated as equivalent to the original: it allows the original document to be admitted as proof of its contents despite the fact that this would otherwise breach the rule against hearsay.

Essential Facts

- According to Dickson, "a party must adduce the best attainable evidence of the facts he means to prove". This is no longer considered a principle of general application, but is of importance in respect of real evidence, and in respect of documentary evidence to a lesser extent.

- As regards real evidence, secondary evidence is competent if it is not reasonably practicable and convenient to produce the primary evidence.
- Even where secondary evidence is competent, a failure to allow the other party to examine the primary evidence may lead to prejudice.
- In civil proceedings, there are statutory provisions providing that "authenticated copies" of documents are to be treated for evidential purposes as if they were the documents themselves, meaning that the "best evidence" rule will not prohibit their use (Civil Evidence (Scotland) Act 1988, s 6).
- Similar, although not identical, provisions apply in criminal proceedings (Criminal Procedure (Scotland) Act 1995, s 279 and Sch 8, para, 1).

Essential Cases

Anderson v Laverock (1976): it was permissible to use secondary evidence of fish in a criminal trial, due to perishability and difficulties of retention. However, the failure to allow the defence to examine them before disposal was prejudicial and meant that A's conviction had to be quashed.

McGowan v Belling (1983): evidence based on an examination of an electric heater was excluded because the heater was still available but not produced in court.

McKellar v Normand (1992): "secondary evidence" is permissible where it would not result in prejudice to the accused.

7 CONFESSIONS AND STATEMENTS AGAINST INTEREST

In a criminal case, one of the most important exceptions to the rule against hearsay (discussed in full in Chapter 5) is the rule that "statements against interest" – or confessions – are admissible.

Although such statements are admissible as an exception to the rule against hearsay, they may be inadmissible on another ground – that is, that the confession was unfairly obtained. This is a complex topic on which there is a considerable body of case law (unsurprisingly, given the potential importance of the issue to persons charged with criminal offences). That body of law is set out in this chapter.

This chapter is concerned only with the admissibility of confessions in criminal procedure. Statements against interest are also admissible in civil procedure, although now that the rule against hearsay has been abolished in civil cases (Civil Evidence (Scotland) Act 1988, s 2(1)), there is no need for any "exception" to the hearsay rule to justify this. It is possible that the use of a statement against interest might be objected to in a civil case on the basis that it was unfairly obtained, but the point has received little attention from the courts (see *Walkers on Evidence* (3rd edn, 2009), para 9.10.1).

What is a confession?

A confession, for the purposes of this chapter, is a statement made by the accused which in some way incriminates him. This need not be a full confession, admitting the criminal allegation in its entirety. It might be incriminating in a much more limited way – for example, a suspect might deny the crime but admit that he had been at the scene of the crime shortly before a witness saw the crime taking place. That statement would be a "statement against interest", admissible as an exception to the hearsay rule, and is subject to the same rules of fairness as a confession. (Indeed, "statement against interest" may be more appropriate as a general term, but "confession" is the term which is normally used and that practice is repeated throughout this chapter for convenience.)

When will a confession be inadmissible?

Access to legal advice

Until recently, suspects in Scotland had no right for a solicitor to be present when interviewed by the police, and the Scottish courts had held this to be compatible with the European Convention on Human Rights (*HM Advocate* v *McLean* (2010)). The Supreme Court, however, decided in *Cadder* v *HM Advocate* (2011) that access to legal advice was required by the European Convention on Human Rights. As a result, any admissions made by a suspect who was denied access to legal advice will be inadmissible in evidence. However, further evidence which the police discover as a result of such an interview will not necessarily be inadmissible, although it would be possible to argue that it should be excluded on grounds of fairness (*HM Advocate* v *P* (2011)).

The right to legal advice can be waived by the suspect, but the waiver must be free, voluntary and informed (*McGowan* v *B* (2012)). The right to access to a lawyer will normally arise when a person is taken into police custody. However, where the individual's freedom to act is otherwise impaired – as, for example, when a person was handcuffed during a drugs search (*Ambrose* v *Harris* (2011)) – any questioning by the police without access to legal advice will be equally inappropriate and any replies to questions inadmissible.

The basic test

Assuming that a suspect was provided with (or waived his right to access) legal advice, then the basic test for deciding whether a confession is admissible or inadmissible is one of "fairness". It has been remarked that this test cuts both ways:

> "While the law of Scotland has always very properly regarded fairness to an accused person as being an integral part of the administration of justice, fairness is not a unilateral consideration. Fairness to the public is also a legitimate consideration, and in so far as police officers in the exercise of their duties are prosecuting and protecting the public interest, it is the function of the Court to seek to provide a proper balance to secure that the rights of individuals are properly preserved, while not hamstringing the police in their investigation of crime with a series of academic vetoes which ignore the realities and practicalities of the situation and discount completely the public interest." (*Miln* v *Cullen* (1967), per the Lord Justice-Clerk (Wheatley) at 29–30)

"Fairness" is not simply a question of whether the police (or other investigators) have acted in good faith. For example, in *Jack* v *HM Advocate*

(1999), the accused was alleged to have "confessed" to a police officer during a break in his trial for child sexual offences, when she said how awful it must be to have such serious allegations made against him if nothing had happened. The court noted that the police officer had no intention of provoking a response, and that she had not wished to give evidence of what the accused had said to her. Nevertheless, it was clearly unfair for such questioning to have taken place while the accused was on trial, and so the evidence of what he had said to the police officer was inadmissible.

One reason for excluding unfairly obtained confessions is that they may be unreliable – for example, people may falsely confess if undue pressure is applied, or if they are not in a position to understand or judge their responses to questions properly. However, confessions may be excluded as unfairly obtained even where there is little or no doubt as to their reliability. The justification for such exclusion probably lies in the protection of what might be termed the "moral integrity" of the criminal process, a concept discussed in more detail in Chapter 8.

The procedure involved in determining admissibility – which may involve what is referred to as a "trial within a trial" – is outlined at the end of this chapter.

Factors which are relevant in determining fairness

There is no closed list of factors which may be taken into account in determining "fairness", but the following have been identified as particularly important (especially the first):

- *The manner of questioning.* In *Lord Advocate's Reference (No 1 of 1983)* (1984), the court said (at 58) that "improper forms of bullying or pressure designed to break the will of the suspect or to force from him a confession against his will" will render a confession inadmissible. (Some earlier cases say that a confession obtained by "cross-examination" is inadmissible, but in this context the term "cross-examination" must be given a meaning along the lines suggested in the *Reference*.)

- *The use of a caution.* If the police suspect an individual of having committed a criminal offence, they may be required to "caution" him – that is, advise him of his right to silence – before questioning him. Whether a caution is required or not depends on the "stage" of the police investigation, and this is discussed further below.

- *The use of threats or inducements.* This will generally result in evidence of a confession being excluded. In *Harley v HM Advocate* (1996), the police told a suspect that if he did not confess they would go to speak to a woman with whom he was having an affair, with the consequence that her husband would become aware of this. It was held that the confession which he gave thereafter was inadmissible. But, by contrast, it was held in *Stewart* v *Hingston* (1997) that a suspect's statement was admissible despite the fact that she had been told that she would be detained and a social worker asked to look after her children if she did not make a statement immediately. The basis for the decision seems to have been that the police officer had acted in good faith and was only explaining what would inevitably have to happen.

- *The fact that the suspect was intoxicated at the time the statement was made.* Although the courts have accepted that this can be a relevant factor, they have been reluctant to exclude evidence on this basis if it appears that the suspect understood what they were saying (*Thomson* v *HM Advocate* (1989)).

- *Mental impairment or illness* on the part of the suspect is a relevant factor, but, again, the courts have been reluctant to exclude evidence on this basis (see, for example, *Higgins* v *HM Advocate* (1993)).

- *The physical condition* of the suspect is relevant. In *McClory* v *MacInnes* (1992) the accused was woken up in his car and asked questions by the police while he was not fully awake: the sheriff excluded evidence of his replies as having been unfairly obtained and this was upheld on appeal.

- *Language difficulties.* In *HM Advocate* v *Olsson* (1941), a suspect with limited English made a confession without an interpreter being present. It was held that his confession was inadmissible (partly because of the lack of an interpreter, and partly because he had not been informed of his right to consult a solicitor).

- *The age of the suspect* is accepted as a relevant factor (see, for example, *Codona* v *HM Advocate* (1996)). For example, lengthy questioning of a young suspect without a break may become "unfair" more quickly than it would in the case of an adult.

Statements to the police: the stage of the investigation

As is noted above, a confession made to the police may be considered to have been unfairly obtained if the police have not cautioned the individual first. Furthermore, once the police have charged a suspect with a crime they should not question him about that allegation at all.

The different stages of the investigatory process (for this purpose) are as follows:

Stage 1: where the individual is not a suspect. Where the police do not suspect an individual as having committed a crime, they may question him without administering a caution. This applies even if that individual has been accused by a member of the public of having committed a crime (as in *Miln* v *Cullen* (1967)).

Stage 2: where the individual has become a suspect. Where an individual has become a suspect, the police should caution him that he is not obliged to say anything and that anything he does say may be recorded and used in evidence (*Tonge* v *HM Advocate* (1982)). If such a caution is not given, then any confession made thereafter will normally be taken to have been unfairly obtained (*HM Advocate* v *Docherty* (1981)). However, this remains a question of fairness and is not an absolute rule – for example, in *Wilson* v *Heywood* (1989), the accused had already been cautioned in relation to another offence. The court took the view that this meant he must have been aware of his right to silence, and so his confession had not been unfairly obtained. At this stage, a failure to provide the suspect with access to legal advice is likely to render any replies inadmissible because of the breach of his Convention rights which will have occurred, as discussed earlier in this chapter.

Stage 3: the individual is charged with an offence. Where the police formally charge a person with an offence, they should administer a caution first. If the accused makes a reply to the charge, then that reply is normally admissible in evidence, but only if a caution was administered (*Tonge* v *HM Advocate* (1982)). The Lord Justice-General (Emslie) explained in *Tonge* (at 140) that the police could not evade the requirement of a caution before charge by avoiding the "formal language of a charge":

> "The reading of a charge is calculated to provoke a response from the accused and it is quite essential that he should know, in advance, of his right to silence, and of the use which may be made of any response which he chooses to make. To charge an accused person without cautioning him is to put pressure upon him which may induce a response, and I have no doubt that by accusing Gray [one of Tonge's co-accused], although not in the formal language of a charge, the accusation was clearly calculated, as a formal charge is calculated, to induce a response from the person accused. The accusation placed pressure upon Gray and I am persuaded that, since no caution was administered before it was made, it is impossible to regard

the statement made in response to it as spontaneous and voluntary. It was plainly induced by the accusation and in the circumstances was induced by unfair means."

Once the suspect has been charged, the police may no longer question him and any replies to questions will be inadmissible. However, it is permissible for the police to question the suspect about other matters (*Carmichael* v *Boyd* (1993)). A suspect who has been charged may indicate that he wishes to make a voluntary statement: this is permissible, but the statement should normally be taken by an officer unconnected with the investigation (see *Tonge* v *HM Advocate*).

Because charging a suspect precludes further questioning, the police may choose to delay proceeding from "stage 2" to "stage 3" in order to question an accused further. It is now clear that the police are permitted to do this, and putting off charging what is sometimes called a "chargeable suspect" does not render answers to questions inadmissible (*Murphy* v *HM Advocate* (1975)). In *HM Advocate* v *Penders* (1996), it was held acceptable for the police to question a suspect even after he had been told that he *would* be charged, although the questioning was in response to a confession by the suspect made after he had been told this.

Statements to persons other than the police

Confessions may, of course, be made not only to police officers, but to a variety of public and private individuals, such as television licence inspectors or store detectives. It has been accepted that the admissibility of such statements may still be objected to on the basis that they have been unfairly obtained (*Pennycuick* v *Lees* (1992)). The courts have, however, laid stress on the fact that persons in these roles may not know how to administer a caution (*Irving* v *Jessop* (1988)). Consequently, it seems that it will generally be difficult to object to the admissibility of statements obtained as a result of questioning by such persons.

Statements overheard or intercepted

It has been held that evidence of statements overheard between suspects held in police custody is admissible. In *Jamieson* v *Annan* (1988), two persons charged in theft were detained in separate cells, and then started a conversation. A police officer heard it and called other police officers to listen in. The evidence of the (incriminatory) statements made by the persons in custody was held admissible. The same principle probably applies to overheard statements generally, but the general "fairness" test might rule out the use of statements obtained by eavesdropping in circumstances where the individuals concerned had a greater expectation of privacy.

The position is different where the police have in some way engineered the making of incriminatory statements, and in *HM Advocate v Higgins* (2006), where the police deliberately placed suspects in adjoining cells and posted officers to listen in on their conversations, the evidence of what was overheard was held to be inadmissible. A further example is *HM Advocate v Campbell* (1964), where a policeman (under the pretence of being a reporter) accompanied an actual reporter to an interview with a suspect, who incriminated himself. The trial judge ruled that evidence of the incriminatory statement was not admissible. The logic of this decision seems to be that if the police had interviewed the suspect directly they would have been obliged to caution him. They could not, therefore, use a third party to question him without a caution, even though the meeting had been instigated by the suspect contacting the reporter and the undercover policeman had simply gone along to a pre-arranged meeting.

Campbell is open to criticism on the basis that the statement was one which the suspect had volunteered to make (see *Weir v Jessop (No 2)* (1991), per the Lord Justice-Clerk (Ross) at 152). However, it would clearly not be proper for the police to engage a third party to question a suspect when they could not do so themselves without administering a caution, and evidence obtained in that way would be inadmissible (as in *HM Advocate v Graham* (1991)).

It should be noted that if the police are to carry out "surveillance" – roughly speaking, a plan of monitoring, observing, or listening to people and their conversations – then this is now likely to require authorisation under the procedures set out in the Regulation of Investigatory Powers (Scotland) Act 2000. A failure to follow these procedures does not, however, automatically render any evidence obtained thereby inadmissible (*Gilchrist v HM Advocate* (2005)), and the common law fairness test will continue to be applicable.

The commission of a crime itself: entrapment

In *Weir v Jessop (No 2)* (1991), the appeal court observed that there was a difference between questioning someone about a crime and eavesdropping on a crime as it was being committed: as long as there was no pressure or inducement to commit the crime, the latter was perfectly legitimate and there was no need to "caution" the suspects.

However, if the police actually *encourage* the commission of a crime, then that might be regarded as improper "entrapment". Some form of pressure is required – it would not be entrapment to simply make a request that the accused commit a crime, such as asking a licensee to serve a drink after permitted hours or asking someone if they have drugs for sale, as in *HM Advocate* v *Harper* (1989).

For some time, the Scottish courts dealt with the issue of entrapment by ruling that evidence obtained in this way would be inadmissible. However, that is an unsatisfactory solution to the problem, because once a person has been entrapped into committing a crime it may be possible to use evidence other than that obtained by the "entrapper" personally in order to secure a conviction. The remedy of excluding evidence may, therefore, have arbitrary and inconsistent results.

It has now been decided (in *Brown* v *HM Advocate* (2002)) that a claim of entrapment need not be dealt with in this way. Instead, an accused can plead entrapment as a bar to their being tried for the alleged crime (see, for example, *Jones* v *HM Advocate* (2010)). Such a plea will, however, succeed only in exceptional circumstances: when the conduct of the police was "so seriously improper as to bring the administration of justice into disrepute" (*R* v *Looseley* (2001), per Lord Nicholls of Birkenhead at para 25).

Statements which an individual is compelled to make under statute

Normally, a person cannot be compelled to make any statement which might incriminate him. However, there are a number of statutory provisions which restrict this "privilege against self-incrimination" and compel persons to provide information. Some of these provisions may state that any information obtained in this way is not admissible in evidence against the person questioned at a later trial or at least restrict such use (see, for example, s 2(8) of the Criminal Justice Act 1987), but this is not always the case.

An example of such a provision is s 172 of the Road Traffic Act 1988, which allows the police to require the owner of a vehicle to state who was driving it at the time an offence was committed. It may well be, for obvious reasons, that the owner will have to incriminate himself in response to such a question. In *Brown* v *Stott* (2001), it was held that this did not breach Art 6 of the European Convention on Human Rights (the right to a fair trial) and that an incriminating answer by the driver could be used against them in court.

It is possible for an accused to argue that a statement made under statutory compulsion should be inadmissible as having been unfairly obtained (*Styr* v *HM Advocate* (1993)), but this will be difficult to establish given that there is an obligation to answer questions in such circumstances. For that reason, there is no need to administer a caution before asking such questions: indeed, given that a caution is a warning to the accused that he need not answer questions, a caution is not only unnecessary, but also inappropriate.

Determining admissibility: the "trial within a trial"

Until recently, it was thought that the question of whether a confession was admissible was a question of fact for the jury. Accordingly, unless the judge was satisfied that no reasonable jury could hold that the confession had been fairly obtained, the court was obliged to admit the evidence and leave it to the jury to decide whether it had been fairly obtained (*Balloch* v *HM Advocate* (1977)). The theory is that the jury could, if it felt the confession had been unfairly obtained, leave it out of consideration, but this is obviously open to objection as being unrealistic.

In the leading case of *Thompson* v *Crowe* (2000), it was held that this approach was incorrect, and that the admissibility of a confession was a matter for the trial judge and not the jury. If the circumstances in which the confession was obtained are in dispute, then the judge should hear evidence on those – outwith the presence of the jury – before deciding the point. Such a procedure is referred to as a "trial within a trial", although it can in fact take place before the trial has even started if the admissibility of a confession has been identified in advance as being an area of dispute.

In summary procedure, where there is no jury, then the judge can simply hear evidence of the confession and any relevant surrounding circumstances in order to determine the question of admissibility. It will be assumed that the judge can disregard the confession if it is inadmissible.

If the admissibility of the confession is in dispute, then it is for the Crown to prove that it was fairly obtained. It need, however, only prove this on the balance of probabilities (*Platt* v *HM Advocate* (2004)).

Essential Facts

- Confessions – or "statements against interest" – by the accused are admissible in a criminal trial under an exception to the rule against hearsay. However, they will be *inadmissible* if they have been unfairly obtained.

- The basic test of admissibility is one of fairness, which involves a consideration of both fairness to the accused and fairness to the public – that is, a consideration of the public interest in the detection of crime.
- In considering fairness, the courts will have regard to all the factors surrounding the confession. Particularly important factors include the manner in which the accused was questioned, the use of a caution, the use of threats or inducements, the physical and mental condition and the age of the accused.
- Where an individual has become a suspect, the police may question him but should caution him that he is not obliged to say anything and that anything he does say may be recorded and given in evidence against him. A failure to do so may render any confession inadmissible.
- Where the police charge a person with a criminal offence, they should not question him further about that offence. If they do, any answers are likely to be inadmissible.
- Statements against interest which are overheard or intercepted are normally admissible in evidence. The police may eavesdrop on the commission of a crime but should not "entrap" a person into committing one.
- Where the admissibility of a confession is challenged, admissibility is a question of law for the judge and not a question of fact for the jury.

Essential Cases

Cadder v HM Advocate (2010): a suspect who is interviewed by the police must have access to legal advice (although this right can be waived by the suspect). If the right of access to legal advice is denied, any answers to questions will be inadmissible.

HM Advocate v Campbell (1964): where a plain-clothes policeman, posing as a reporter, accompanied an actual reporter who went to question a suspect, this was unfair and rendered the suspect's confession inadmissible. This was doubted by Lord Ross in *Weir* v *Jessop (No 2)* (1991).

HM Advocate v Higgins (2006): the police placed suspects in adjoining cells and posted officers to listen in to their conversations. The evidence obtained thereby was held to be inadmissible.

Jamieson v Annan (1988): statements shouted between two persons in different police cells and overheard by the police were heard admissible in evidence.

Lord Advocate's Reference (No 1 of 1983) (1984): "improper forms of bullying or pressure designed to break the will of the suspect or to force from him a confession against his will" will render a confession inadmissible.

Miln v Cullen (1967): in applying the "fairness" test, the courts must have regard to both fairness to the accused and fairness to the public.

Thompson v Crowe (2000): the admissibility of a confession is a question of law for the judge and not a question of fact for the jury. If it is necessary to hear evidence to establish the circumstances in which the confession was obtained, this should be done by way of a "trial within a trial" outwith the presence of the jury.

Tonge v HM Advocate (1982): where an individual has become a suspect, the police should caution him before questioning him.

8 IMPROPERLY OBTAINED REAL AND DOCUMENTARY EVIDENCE

Where a party wishes to rely on real or documentary evidence in court, it may be objected to on the ground that it has not been lawfully obtained. If the evidence has been improperly obtained, a criminal court has a discretion to either admit or refuse to admit it (*Lawrie* v *Muir* (1950)). This discretion to excuse an illegality is necessary only where there has been a breach of the legal rules governing investigative action. Other illegalities do not in themselves affect the admissibility of evidence. So, in *Howard* v *HM Advocate* (2006), where a landlady gathered together her tenant's belongings, and found cannabis resin, it was held that her actions did not amount to an unlawful search and so there was no illegality to excuse. The fact that she had been acting unlawfully (and probably committing a criminal offence under s 22 of the Rent (Scotland) Act 1984) in attempting to evict her tenant without a court action was irrelevant.

Before discussing the discretion to admit improperly obtained evidence it is necessary to set out the circumstances in which such evidence can be lawfully obtained – either by a lawful search or with the consent of the person from whom the evidence is obtained. If evidence has been obtained lawfully, there is no need to consider the court's discretion.

Most of this chapter is concerned with the admissibility of such evidence in criminal proceedings. There is very little authority on the exclusion of improperly obtained evidence in civil proceedings, but the position is outlined briefly at the end of this chapter.

Evidence obtained by a lawful search

Search pursuant to a warrant

Where the police wish to conduct a search, they may apply for a warrant, which is normally granted by a sheriff or a justice of the peace. The warrant will specify the terms of the search that may be carried out. Warrants may be granted at common law or under a variety of statutory provisions.

Warrants are not restricted to premises, and may be obtained to search, or take samples/impressions from, an individual. The leading case is *Hay* v *HM Advocate* (1968), where, during a murder investigation, it was observed that a youth's bite appeared similar to marks on the deceased. It was held that it was competent for the Crown to obtain a warrant for the youth to be taken to a dental hospital for dental surgeons to take an impression of his teeth to confirm this.

Was the warrant valid? A warrant must be appropriately signed, dated, and identify the subject of the search. If not signed, it will be invalid (*HM Advocate* v *Bell* (1985)). As regards the other aspects, the basic question is whether the person who is shown the warrant will be able to satisfy themselves that the bearer has authority to conduct the search. So, in *Bell* v *HM Advocate* (1988), it was held sufficient that the warrant referred to the "said premises" in the warrant, because these were clearly identified in the information on oath which preceded it.

Dates (or the lack of dates) on warrants have caused further problems, but these can be resolved by asking the same question. In *Bulloch* v *HM Advocate* (1980), warrants were granted under statutory powers which required the warrants to be executed within 14 days. They were dated "September 1976" only, and the search took place on 30 September. Accordingly, it would have been impossible for someone reading the warrant to satisfy himself that the search was authorised, and so the search was held to have been unlawful. This does not mean, however, that a precise date is always essential: in *HM Advocate* v *Foulis* (2002), a warrant dated by month and year only was held to be valid, because it was a common law warrant and not subject to strict time limits such as that found in *Bulloch*.

Was the search within the scope of the warrant? The fact that a warrant has been granted does not entitle the police to search for items outwith the scope of the warrant – see, for example, *HM Advocate* v *Turnbull* (1951), where a warrant was granted to search the office of an accountant accused of making fraudulent tax returns on behalf of a particular client. The police removed a large number of files relating to other clients. It was held that this was illegal and that the documents could not be used in evidence against the accused.

By contrast, if police officers "accidentally [stumble] upon evidence of a plainly incriminating character in the course of a search for a different purpose", they may take possession of the relevant items and they will be admissible in evidence (the quote is from *HM Advocate* v *Hepper* (1958), per Lord Guthrie at 40).

The distinction is illustrated by *Drummond* v *HM Advocate* (1992), where a warrant was granted to search for stolen furniture. During the search, two police officers, searching together, found stolen clothes – from a break-in at the "Crystal Works" – in a wardrobe. One of the officers gave evidence that he had been looking for items stolen from the Crystal Works, while a second gave evidence that he had been looking for small items of furniture. It was held that the evidence of the second police officer was admissible, but that the evidence of the first was not.

Search without warrant under statute

In some circumstances, the police (or other public officials) may be given powers of search under statute which do not require a warrant to be obtained. An example is s 23(2) of the Misuse of Drugs Act 1971, which provides that a police officer who "has reasonable grounds to suspect that any person is in possession of a controlled drug" may search that person, or any vehicle or vessel in which he suspects the drug may be found.

There are similar statutory powers under ss 48, 49B and 50 of the Criminal Law (Consolidation) (Scotland) Act 1995, permitting police officers to search for offensive weapons where they have reasonable grounds to believe that a person has such items in their possession unlawfully. Another example is s 60 of the Civic Government (Scotland) Act 1982, giving police officers powers of search without warrant where they have reasonable grounds to suspect that a person is in possession of stolen property.

Where a person has been arrested or detained, there are further powers under s 18 of the Criminal Procedure (Scotland) Act 1995. In such circumstances, a police officer may take "relevant physical data" – such as fingerprints, palm prints or impressions of another part of the body – from the individual concerned, and also samples of hair, nails, body fluid or body tissue. "Reasonable force" may normally be used to enforce these provisions (see s 19B of the Act), although in some circumstances the approval of a senior police officer is required.

Search without warrant in circumstances of urgency

In circumstances of urgency, it may be legitimate to conduct a search without a warrant or statutory authorisation. The leading case is *HM Advocate* v *McGuigan* (1936), where the accused was charged with murder, rape and theft by the police, who then searched the tent where he lived with his mother and stepfather. In allowing the evidence obtained to be admitted, the Lord Justice-Clerk (Aitchison) said that, as the matter had been viewed by the police as "one of urgency", they were entitled to conduct the search without a warrant.

A more recent example is provided by *Edgley* v *Barbour* (1995), where the police suspected a driver to be using an illegal radar detection device. They stopped his car – around midnight in a remote location –

whereupon he denied having such a device. One police officer then opened the passenger door and the glove compartment where he found the device. The sheriff admitted the evidence, holding that it was "quite impracticable" to expect the police officers to obtain a warrant, as such a procedure would have given the driver ample time to dispose of the device which they had good reason to believe was in the vehicle. The sheriff's decision was upheld on appeal.

Evidence obtained by consent

In some circumstances, a person may voluntarily comply with a request by a police officer – either to allow the officer to conduct a search, or a request to hand items over. There is no need for a warrant in such circumstances, although if the person is suspected of a crime then they should be cautioned that they are not obliged to comply (*Davidson* v *Brown* (1990)). In *Mackintosh* v *Scott* (1999), evidence obtained by a nightclub doorman who had told a patron to turn out his pockets (which contained 11 ecstasy tablets) was held to be admissible. The court said that there was no need for a caution given that the doorman was a lay person and not a police officer.

What if the evidence has been improperly obtained?

The fact that evidence has been improperly obtained does not auto-matically make it inadmissible in court: "an irregularity in the obtaining of evidence does not necessarily make that evidence inadmissible" (*HM Advocate* v *McGuigan* (1936), per the Lord Justice-Clerk (Aitchison) at 18). In deciding whether to admit the evidence, the courts will have to apply the "balancing test" famously set out in *Lawrie* v *Muir* (1950), which is worth quoting in full. The Lord Justice-General (Cooper) said (at 26–27):

> "From the standpoint of principle it seems to me that the law must strive to reconcile two highly important interests which are liable to come into conflict – (a) the interest of the citizen to be protected from illegal or irregular invasions of his liberties by the authorities, and (b) the interest of the State to secure that evidence bearing upon the commission of crime and necessary to enable justice to be done shall not be withheld from Courts of law on any merely formal or technical ground. Neither of these objects can be insisted upon to the uttermost. The protection of the citizen is primarily protection for the innocent citizen against unwarranted, wrongful and perhaps high-handed interference, and the common sanction is an action of damages. The protection is not intended

as a protection for the guilty citizen against the efforts of the public prosecutor to vindicate the law. On the other hand, the interest of the State cannot be magnified to the point of causing all the safeguards for the protection of the citizen to vanish, and of offering a positive inducement to the authorities to proceed by irregular methods."

Why should the courts consider excluding such evidence at all? As noted in Chapter 7, one possible reason for excluding improperly obtained admissions and confessions is that they may be unreliable because of the circumstances in which they were obtained. But that problem is much less acute – if it is a problem at all – where real or documentary evidence is concerned.

One common justification for excluding such evidence is that it will deter the police and other investigatory authorities from inappropriate behaviour. As the Lord-Justice General (Cooper) put it in *McGovern v HM Advocate* (1950), at 37: "unless the principles under which police investigations are carried out are adhered to with reasonable strictness, the anchor of the entire system for the protection of the public will very soon begin to drag". It is, however, generally acknowledged that this rationale is unconvincing: any "deterrent" effect is likely to be weak at best given that the exclusion of evidence is likely to occur in only a small proportion of cases and has no guaranteed consequences for the police officer(s) who carried out the initial investigation. Indeed, it is the public interest in seeing crime punished which is more likely to suffer from the exclusion of evidence.

Instead, the justification for excluding such evidence probably lies in protecting what has been termed the "moral integrity" of the criminal justice process. (See further P Duff, "Admissibility of improperly obtained physical evidence in the Scottish criminal trial: the search for principle" (2004) 8 Edin LR 152.) Always to exclude improperly obtained evidence would lead the criminal justice system into disrepute, by allowing clearly guilty (and frequently dangerous) offenders to walk free from court; but always to admit it would similarly damage the process and provide little protection for the rights of persons suspected of crime. The courts must steer a middle course in line with the "balancing test" outlined in *Lawrie v Muir*.

Applying the "balancing test" in practice

There is no fixed list of factors which a court may take into account in applying the "balancing test", but the following are some factors which have been identified as being of particular importance:

- *How serious is the crime charged?* In *Lawrie* v *Muir* itself, Lord Cooper remarked that it was easy to see why a departure from the rules of investigation might be held to be fatal to the prosecution case where the accused was charged with a technical regulatory offence, but observed (at 27) that "it would usually be wrong to exclude some highly incriminating production in a murder trial merely because it was found by a police officer in the course of a search authorised for a different purpose or before a proper warrant had been obtained". This is controversial, however, in that it suggests that the more serious the allegation, the less important it is to respect the rights of the accused.

- *Did the investigators act in good faith?* In *Fairley* v *Fishmongers of London* (1951), a private inspector and a Ministry of Food official discovered that the accused was in possession of a large number of unclean and unseasonable salmon (which was a statutory offence under s 20 of the Salmon Fisheries (Scotland) Act 1868). They had not, however obtained the necessary search warrant under s 26 of that Act. In holding that the evidence should be admitted despite the irregularity, Lord Cooper remarked (at 24) that the inspectors had acted in good faith and that there was "nothing to suggest that any departure from the strict procedure was deliberately adopted with a view to securing the admission of evidence obtained by an unfair trick".

- *Were there circumstances of urgency?* As noted above, a search without warrant may be lawful because of circumstances of urgency. It seems also that a search may be regarded as irregular but circumstances of urgency relied upon to justify the court exercising its discretion to admit the evidence. In *Walsh* v *MacPhail* (1978), cannabis resin was found in the appellant's room at the RAF base in Edzell. The search had been based on a purported warrant granted by a senior officer at the base which was not in fact valid. In holding that the evidence obtained was nevertheless admissible, the court laid stress on both the good faith of those conducting the search, and the circumstances of urgency (in that delay might have resulted in the drugs being removed and disposed of).

- *Was the irregularity trivial?* In *McGovern* v *HM Advocate* (1950), the accused was suspected of breaking into an office and blowing open a safe with explosives. Without his consent or a warrant, the police took scrapings from his fingernails, which showed traces of explosives. The appeal court remarked that "relative triviality" of an irregularity might be a reason for excluding it, but considered that the irregularity here was not trivial: the police had been able to follow the correct procedure in obtaining a warrant to search McGovern's house and should easily have been able to adopt the appropriate procedure in relation to searching his person.

Improperly obtained evidence and the ECHR

Where evidence has been improperly obtained, this will frequently amount to a breach of Art 8 of the European Convention on Human Rights, on the basis that there has been an interference with the right to respect for private and family life which is not "in accordance with the law". In terms of the ECHR itself, all this means is that Art 8 has been breached and that the individual can pursue appropriate remedies. It does not prevent the evidence being used, unless its use also breaches Art 6 (the right to a fair trial), which is not an automatic consequence of a breach of Art 8 (see *Khan* v *UK* (2001)).

However, in Scotland, the Lord Advocate (or a procurator fiscal) has no power to do anything which is "incompatible" with Convention rights (Scotland Act 1998, s 57(2)). For some time, it was argued that this meant that the Crown could not use evidence in court if it had been obtained in breach of Art 8 (see, for example, *Connor* v *HM Advocate* (2002)). The point was settled in *McGibbon* v *HM Advocate* (2004), where it was held that s 57(2) does not have this effect. The ECHR and the Scotland Act 1998 do not, therefore, have the effect of automatically barring the Crown from using improperly obtained evidence, and the "balancing test" set out in *Lawrie* v *Muir* remains the appropriate approach.

Improperly obtained evidence in civil cases

There is no established rule precluding the use of improperly obtained evidence in civil cases, although there is only a limited amount of case law addressing the point. The leading case is *Rattray* v *Rattray* (1897), a divorce action where the pursuer sought to rely on a letter written by the defender (his wife) to the co-defender (her alleged lover). By a majority, the Inner House held that the letter was admissible in evidence despite the circumstances in which it had been obtained (it was stolen from the Post Office, a crime which had resulted in the pursuer being imprisoned for a short period). It is important to note that the court's decision rested on a somewhat peculiar view that this was not really a crime. Lord Trayner said (at 318):

"I think the pursuer's act can scarcely be regarded as crime, in the ordinary sense of the word. He committed a statutory offence, unquestionably, but so does the man who refuses to have his child vaccinated, or gives false information to the Registrar of Births ... none of these offences is regarded as 'crime' in its popular sense. I think the pursuer intercepted a letter not his own in the hands of the Post-office authorities ... but I cannot regard this as the same case, or leading to the same consequence, as that of a man ... who breaks into his neighbour's desk or safe and abstracts documents therefrom."

Rattray has been criticised occasionally, and was considered further in the later case of *Duke of Argyll* v *Duchess of Argyll* (1963). In that case, also a divorce action, the pursuer sought to prove adultery by relying on his wife's diaries, which he had obtained by breaking into her house when they were living apart. Lord Wheatley suggested that, bearing in mind that adultery was historically a quasi-criminal offence which required (at the time) to be proven beyond reasonable doubt in a divorce action, it was appropriate to apply the *Lawrie* v *Muir* test to decide whether the evidence could be admitted. The result was the same as in *Rattray* – the evidence was admitted – but this case may suggest a different approach to improperly obtained evidence in civil cases. That said, it rests particularly on the unusual status of adultery in a civil action at the time and may be an isolated decision.

Essential Facts

Criminal cases

- Real and documentary evidence which has been irregularly obtained is not necessarily inadmissible in court – the court has a discretion either to admit it or to refuse to do so.

Obtaining evidence by regular means

- Evidence can be regularly obtained either by a lawful search or with the consent of the person from whom it is obtained.
- A lawful search should normally take place pursuant to a warrant.
- Warrants are normally granted to search premises, but may also be granted to search a person or take samples or impressions from them.
- A warrant should be signed and dated and identify the subjects to be searched. Minor errors in the description or an incomplete date may be excused provided that the warrant still contains sufficient information

to enable the person who is being searched to satisfy themselves that the warrant grants the necessary permission.

- If police officers deliberately go beyond the scope of the warrant, evidence obtained thereby will be inadmissible. However, if they accidentally come across some incriminating material during a search for another purpose, they may take possession of it and it will be admissible in evidence.
- Search without warrant is authorised under statute in certain circumstances, and may also be justified in circumstances of urgency.

Admitting improperly obtained evidence

- Evidence which has been improperly obtained is not necessarily inadmissible.
- In deciding whether to admit improperly obtained evidence, the court will balance the interests of the individual against the interests of the state in the detection and prosecution of crime.
- In applying that "balancing test", the court will consider factors such as the seriousness of the crime charged, whether the investigators acted in good faith, and the seriousness of the irregularity.

Civil cases

- There is very little case law on the use of improperly obtained evidence in civil cases. At present, it appears that there is no prohibition on using such evidence, although this position has been criticised.

Essential Cases

Bulloch v HM Advocate (1980): where a statutory warrant, which had to be executed within 14 days of being granted, was dated "September 1976" only, and executed on 30 September, the search was unlawful.

HM Advocate v Turnbull (1951): where the police were granted a warrant to search the office of an accountant accused of making fraudulent tax returns in respect of a particular client, it was illegal for them to remove files relating to other clients.

Hay v HM Advocate (1968): it was competent to seek a warrant for a man to be taken to a dental hospital for impressions of his teeth to be taken.

Lawrie v Muir (1950): in deciding whether to admit improperly obtained evidence, the court must take into account both the interests of the individual and the interests of the state. This case established this "balancing test".

McGibbon v HM Advocate (2004): evidence which has been obtained in breach of Art 8 of the ECHR (the right to respect for private and family life) is not automatically inadmissible in a Scottish court.

Rattray v Rattray (1897): an unlawfully obtained letter was held to be admissible in a divorce action. Some doubt is cast on this decision by *Duke of Argyll* v *Duchess of Argyll* (1963).

9 CHARACTER AND COLLATERAL EVIDENCE

Evidence which has little bearing on the case in hand may be held inadmissible on the basis that it relates to a "collateral issue", rather than to the facts which have to be decided by the court. In the civil case of *A* v *B* (1895), the pursuer alleged that she had been raped by the defender. In support of her allegation, she sought to prove that he had previously attempted to rape two other women on earlier dates. The Inner House held that she should not be entitled to lead the proposed evidence. The Lord President (Robertson) explained (at 404) that although the evidence was "irrelevant", that was not to say that it had "no bearing at all" on the case:

> "if the defender admitted at the trial that he had attempted to ravish those two other women, I think the jury might legitimately hold that this made it the more likely that he ravished the pursuer. But, then, Courts of law are not bound to admit the ascertainment of every disputed fact which may contribute, however slightly or indirectly, towards the solution of the issue to be tried. Regard must be had to the limitations which time and human liability to confusion impose upon the conduct of all trials. Experience shews that it is better to sacrifice the aid which might be got from the more or less uncertain solution of collateral issues, than to spend a great deal of time, and confuse the jury with what, in the end, even supposing it to be certain, has only an indirect bearing on the matter in hand".

Lord McLaren also remarked (at 405) that if the allegations were true, it would be a "cruel aggravation of the wrong already suffered" to lead evidence from the other women alleged to have been raped, one which he considered to be "without any corresponding benefit to the pursuer's case", given that the evidence could be of indirect benefit at most. That is an illustration of what might be regarded as policy factors – rather than the pure issue of relevance alone – influencing the court's decision to treat the evidence as collateral and therefore inadmissible.

The principal – although not the only – form of collateral evidence is evidence of a person's character. Here, in particular, attention is paid not only to the limited relevance of such evidence – or its lack of "probative value" – but also its prejudicial effect. In the case of accused persons, it is often thought that admitting evidence of matters such as prior convictions may be so prejudicial as to increase unacceptably the risk of wrongful conviction.

This chapter sets out the rules relating to the admissibility of the following types of evidence:

- evidence of prior conduct by the accused at common law;
- evidence of the accused's character under statute;
- evidence of the character of a victim or complainer in criminal proceedings;
- evidence of the character of a witness (in both civil and criminal proceedings);
- collateral evidence in civil proceedings generally.

Prior conduct by the accused: admissibility at common law

In some cases, it may be appropriate to lead evidence of prior (mis)conduct by the accused because it is relevant to prove the crime with which he is charged. Such evidence cannot normally be admitted merely to undermine his credibility.

The principles to be applied here are similar to that recognised under the *Moorov* doctrine (discussed in Chapter 4) whereby evidence of one criminal charge may be used to corroborate evidence of a second criminal charge (and vice versa). In some cases, however, it may be possible to lead evidence of misconduct which does *not* form part of the charge(s) against the accused, provided that it can be shown to be relevant.

For example, in *James Ritchie and Andrew Morren* (1841), two men were convicted of "uttering base coin" – that is, passing false coins off as genuine. The prosecution sought to lead evidence of earlier unsuccessful attempts they had made to pass off coins as genuine, which was objected to. The court ruled that the evidence was admissible, and it is clear that it would have been of considerable importance to the prosecution case as helping to establish that Ritchie and Morren knew well that the coins in their possession were false. (See also *Gallagher* v *Paton* (1909), where the charge was one of fraud and the court allowed evidence of similar false statements made by the accused earlier in the day, and *HM Advocate* v *Joseph* (1929), noted in Chapter 4.)

Although the admissibility of such evidence is closely linked to the *Moorov* doctrine and other rules of corroboration, it is often treated as if it were a separate rule. That approach is reflected in this book – in line with most courses and texts on evidence – but it is not fully defensible as a matter of principle. As noted in Chapter 4, it might be helpful if the Scottish courts were to recognise a single doctrine of "similar fact evidence". In all cases, the underlying question is one of relevance and admissibility: is this evidence admissible to prove a fact in issue?

If the Crown wishes to lead evidence to the effect that the accused has committed a crime with which he is not charged, then it must give fair notice of its intention to do so. This may involve specifying the allegations concerned in the complaint or indictment, which will be necessary if:

> "the evidence sought to be led tends to show that the accused was of bad character, and that other crime is so different in time, place or character from the crime charged that the libel does not give fair notice to the accused that evidence relating to that other crime may be led; or if it is the intention as proof of the crime charged to establish that the accused was in fact guilty of that other crime". (*Nelson* v *HM Advocate* (1994), per the Lord Justice-General (Hope) at 104)

The character of the accused in criminal proceedings: admissibility under statute

Evidence about the character of the accused – including evidence of any previous convictions – is generally prohibited under various rules found in the Criminal Procedure (Scotland) Act 1995, as follows:

Previous convictions
There is a general prohibition against laying evidence of a previous conviction before the court (ss 101 and 166 of the Criminal Procedure (Scotland) Act 1995). This rule is, however, subject to exceptions under ss 266 and 270 (discussed in turn below).

It is also subject to an exception where evidence of a previous conviction is competent as evidence "in support of a substantive charge" (ss 101(2) and 166(b)(i)): for example, if an accused were charged with driving while disqualified, it would be competent to prove that he was convicted of a motoring offence and disqualified as a result. (In practice, such evidence will rarely be necessary: this is an example of an offence alleged to have been committed in a "special capacity" – ie being a disqualified driver – where the special capacity is deemed to have been admitted by the accused unless challenged, meaning that it is normally unnecessary to lead evidence on the point: see s 255 of the 1995 Act.) This exception would also encompass evidence of the type discussed in the prior section as being admissible at common law.

The prohibition applies not simply to explicit evidence of a previous conviction, but also evidence which carries that implication. So, for example, it was held in *Carberry* v *HM Advocate* (1975) that a statement by an accused person that he had got a car from a man he met "when they had both been in Barlinnie" was a reference to a previous conviction, as a jury would be likely to infer from the statement that the accused had been convicted of a crime. However, in that case the statement was a necessary part of the Crown case and so its use did not fall foul of the statutory prohibition.

Because evidence of previous convictions is regarded as particularly prejudicial, if the prohibition is breached this will normally result in the trial diet being deserted or any conviction quashed on appeal (see, for example, *Cordiner* v *HM Advocate* (1978)). However, the appeal court has stressed that a conviction will not automatically be quashed in such circumstances if there is no basis for a finding that there has been a miscarriage of justice (*McCuaig* v *HM Advocate* (1982)); and see also *Cordiner*, per the Lord Justice-Clerk (Wheatley) at 68, suggesting that it could not be considered conceivable that the wrongful disclosure of a conviction for a trivial motoring offence could result in the quashing of a conviction for murder.

Section 266 of the Criminal Procedure (Scotland) Act 1995

Section 266 of the 1995 Act applies where the accused gives evidence on his own behalf. It provides that, as a general rule, the accused "shall not be asked, and if asked shall not be required to answer, any question tending to show that he has committed, or been convicted of, or been charged with, any offence other than that with which he is then charged, or is of bad character" (s 266(4)), but goes on to set out three exceptions to this rule, which apply where:

> "(a) the proof that he has committed or been convicted of such other offence is admissible evidence to show that he is guilty of the offence with which he is then charged; or
> (b) the accused or his counsel or solicitor has asked questions of the witnesses for the prosecution with a view to establishing the accused's good character or impugning the character of the complainer, or the accused has given evidence of his own good character, or the nature or conduct of the defence is such as to involve imputations on the character of the prosecutor or of the witnesses for the prosecution or of the complainer; or
> (c) the accused has given evidence against any other person charged in the same proceedings."

In *Leggate* v *HM Advocate* (1988), where the accused denied having made an incriminating statement to the police, or having shown them where a gun was concealed (he alleged he had been taken by the police to the location). His counsel accepted that his defence involved alleging that the police had conspired to pervert the course of justice. The appeal court held (1) that exception (b) did not apply just because it was asserted that a Crown witness was lying – otherwise in most cases no real defence could be conducted without triggering the exception; (2) that Leggate's case went beyond this and therefore exception (b) *did* apply, but (3) that the court had a discretion not to permit questioning as to bad character even where exception (b) applied.

In *Leggate*, the court ruled that L's conviction had to be quashed because the trial judge had not considered whether to exercise his discretion. However, this should not be taken as indicating that the discretion – had it been exercised – should have been used to prevent L being questioned on his character: in the later case of *Sinclair* v *Macdonald* (1996), where the accused's defence again involved alleging that prosecution witnesses had conspired to make a false allegation, the appeal court held that the trial sheriff had been right to allow the accused to be questioned as to his character.

It should be noted that, although the trial judge has a discretion as to whether or not to allow questioning as to character where exception (b) applies, there is no such discretion where exceptions (a) or (c) apply. (See s 266(5) of the 1995 Act.)

Section 270 of the Criminal Procedure (Scotland) Act 1995

Under s 270 of the 1995 Act, evidence as to the character of the accused may become admissible where either (a) the defence attempts to establish that the accused is of good character or to impugn the character of the prosecutor, complainer or any prosecution witness, or (b) "the nature or conduct of the defence is such as to tend to establish the accused's good character or to involve imputations on the character of the prosecutor, of any witness for the prosecution or of the complainer".

Where one of these conditions is satisfied, the court may "permit the prosecutor to lead evidence that the accused has committed, or has been convicted of, or has been charged with, offences other than that for which he is being tried, or is of bad character" (s 270(2)). The importance of s 270 is that – unlike s 266 – it applies regardless of whether the accused himself gives evidence. It has been observed, however, that it "appears to have been scarcely, if ever, used" (*DS* v *HM Advocate* (2007), per Lord Hope of Craighead at para 32). In practice, s 266 is significantly more important.

The character of a victim or complainer in criminal proceedings

In some circumstances, the accused may seek to lead evidence as to the character of a victim or complainer. These rules are distinct from the rules pertaining to the credibility of a witness (on which, see below), and do not depend on the complainer giving evidence themselves. (Usually, of course, the complainer in a criminal trial will give evidence, but this is not essential – and, of course, deceased victims are in no position to testify.)

There are two circumstances where such evidence may be particularly significant – first, where the accused is charged with a crime of violence and pleads self-defence; and secondly, where the offence is a sexual one and the accused's line of defence is that the complainer consented to the sexual activity.

Murder and other crimes of violence

Where crimes of violence are concerned, there are some older cases which suggest that it is competent – at least where a defence of self-defence is lodged – to prove the "general temper" of the injured person, but not to lead evidence of specific acts of violence which they are alleged to have committed. (See *James Irving* (1838) and *Margaret Fletcher* (1846).) Although that proposition is commonly repeated in the textbooks, it is open to criticism on the very obvious ground that the accused cannot readily be expected to prove that the complainer had a violent disposition without leading evidence of specific acts of violence (Scottish Law Commission, *The Law of Evidence* (Memorandum No 46, 1980), para Q.05).

In one well-known case, *HM Advocate* v *Kay* (1970), the accused was charged with murdering her husband, and the indictment libelled specifically that she had "previously evince[d] malice and ill-will towards him". In light of that specific claim, the trial judge held that she should be entitled to lead evidence of specific assaults on her by him.

Kay does not call the rule against leading evidence of specific acts of violence into doubt. The trial judge in *Kay* specifically described his decision as a "departure from the general rule", and the appeal court has reaffirmed that the general rule remains valid (*Brady* v *HM Advocate* (1986), where *Kay* is described as a "very special case", and see also *Mann, Petitioner* (2001)).

Sexual offences

At common law, the admissibility of what is known as "sexual history" evidence was regarded as a significant exception to the rule against the use of character evidence. As a result, a man charged with a sexual offence could readily lead evidence of prior sexual activity with the complainer, or evidence tending to show that the complainer was of bad character. However, it was not permissible to lead evidence tending to show that the complainer had engaged in specific sexual acts with other men (*Dickie* v *HM Advocate* (1897)).

Over time, the admissibility of such evidence has been restricted by statute, the first such provisions being enacted in 1985 (Law Reform (Miscellaneous Provisions) (Scotland) Act 1985). There has been continuing concern that such restrictions may not be rigorously enforced by courts, and that victims of sexual offences may face unnecessary and distressing questioning as a result. Recently, the statutory rules have been tightened further by the Sexual Offences (Procedure and Evidence) (Scotland) Act 2002, which amends the Criminal Procedure (Scotland) Act 1995.

Section 274(1) of the 1995 Act (as amended) sets out a basic prohibition on the use of "sexual history" evidence, as follows:

"In the trial of a person charged with an offence to which s 288C of this Act applies, the court shall not admit, or allow questioning designed to elicit, evidence which shows or tends to show that the complainer –

(a) is not of good character (whether in relation to sexual matters or otherwise);

(b) has, at any time, engaged in sexual behaviour not forming part of the subject matter of the charge;

(c) has, at any time (other than shortly before, at the same time as or shortly after the acts which form part of the subject matter of the charge), engaged in such behaviour, not being sexual behaviour, as might found the inference that the complainer –

(i) is likely to have consented to those acts; or

(ii) is not a credible or reliable witness; or

(d) has, at any time, been subject to any such condition or predisposition as might found the inference referred to in sub-paragraph (c) above."

This restriction is subject to a procedure under s 275, whereby the court may permit an application to allow such questions. Under s 275(1), however, it can only do so if satisfied that:

"(a) the evidence or questioning will relate only to a specific occurrence or occurrences of sexual or other behaviour, or to specific facts demon-strating –

(i) the complainer's character; or

(ii) any condition or predisposition to which the complainer is or has
been subject;

(b) that occurrence or those occurrences of behaviour or facts are relevant
to establishing whether the accused is guilty of the offence with which he
is charged; and

(c) the probative value of the evidence sought to be admitted or elicited
is significant and is likely to outweigh any risk of prejudice to the proper
administration of justice arising from its being admitted or elicited."

(The comma after "behaviour" does not appear in the 1995 Act, but was
"read into" the legislation by the Privy Council in *DS* v *HM Advocate*
(2007). This means that (i) and (ii) thereafter only qualify the admissibility
of "specific facts" and not evidence of "a specific occurrence or occurrences
of sexual or other behaviour". Evidence of such behaviour will still remain
inadmissible unless the criteria in (b) and (c) are satisfied.)

Decisions to allow or disallow questioning under s 275 will depend
on the facts of individual cases. There have, however, been some controversial decisions, particularly *Kinnin* v *HM Advocate* (2003). In that
case, the appeal court ruled that where K was charged with raping the
complainer, he should have been entitled to have led evidence showing
that the complainer had made a statement indicating that she wished to
have sexual intercourse with K's son. The court's reasons are unclear, but
it should be noted that the accused's argument in support of admitting the
evidence was not based on the relationship between K and his son, but
instead on the premise that the evidence indicated that the complainer
"was a person willing to engage in adulterous relations".

Evidence that a complainer is "generally untruthful" will not qualify,
as it is evidence neither of specific facts, nor of behaviour (*Mackay* v *HM
Advocate* (2005)).

The application to lead such evidence or ask questions of this nature
must be submitted in advance in writing. In *Moir* v *HM Advocate* (2005),
the appeal court rejected an argument that the restrictions on the use
of sexual history evidence were so strict as to run foul of the right to a
fair trial under Art 6 of the European Convention on Human Rights,
pointing out that the judge had a discretion as to whether or not evidence
should be admitted, and that the restrictions were legitimate in order to
protect the complainer's rights under Art 8 (the right to respect for private
and family life).

Where the court grants an application under s 275, any previous
"relevant conviction" of the accused – that is, any prior conviction for
a sexual offence – is laid before the jury (or, in summary proceedings,

taken into consideration by the judge), unless it would be contrary to the "interests of justice" for this to happen. In *DS* v *HM Advocate* (2007), the Privy Council rejected an argument that this rule was contrary to the accused's right to a fair trial under Art 6 ECHR.

The character of a witness

A witness may be cross-examined in an attempt to cast doubt on his credibility, or to show that he has a personal interest in the case (see *Walkers on Evidence* (3rd edn, 2009), para 12.9.3). However:

> "The right to attack the character of a witness, and to bring evidence in support of the attack, is one which has always been carefully kept within very limited bounds. There are two reasons why this should be so. First, it is the duty of a Court to protect witnesses from attacks which they cannot be prepared to meet, and which they can claim no right to meet, by leading evidence to rebut them. And second, such inquiries, if entered upon, would necessarily interfere with the conduct of judicial proceedings by introducing collateral issues, which would be most inconvenient and embarrassing, and might often protract proceedings and obscure the true issue which was being tried." (*Dickie* v *HM Advocate* (1897)), per the Lord Justice-Clerk (Macdonald) at 83)

Accordingly, it seems that while the court will allow a witness to face questions of this nature, it will not be competent to lead evidence challenging the honesty of the witness's response. In *Dickie* the Lord Justice-Clerk stated that if a witness denied having committed a crime, it would not be competent to lead evidence to prove the contrary: the most that could be done would be to produce an extract conviction to contradict the witness's claim. (This is not, of course, to say that a witness can lie with impunity, as dishonest answers could lead to a charge of perjury.) It should be noted that a witness accused of having committed a crime may be entitled to refuse to answer the question, because of the privilege against self-incrimination (see Chapter 10).

There is one specific situation where evidence may, under statute, be led to attack the credibility of a witness. Section 263(4) of the Criminal Procedure (Scotland) Act 1995 provides that "a witness may be examined as to whether he has on any specified occasion made a statement on any matter pertinent to the issue at the trial different from the evidence given by him in the trial; and evidence may be led in the trial to prove that the witness made the different statement on the occasion specified". Where evidence of a prior statement is led under this provision, it is only admissible for the purpose of attacking the credibility of the witness. It is not evidence of the truth of the statement itself (*Paterson* v *HM Advocate* (1974)).

There is a similar statutory provision in civil cases – Evidence (Scotland) Act 1852, s 3 – but this is of limited importance now that the rule against hearsay has been abolished in civil cases (see Chapter 5), meaning that such statements are admissible as proof of their facts in any case.

Collateral evidence in civil proceedings

As *A* v *B* (1895), discussed at the outset of this chapter, demonstrates, collateral evidence is generally inadmissible in civil cases. *A* v *B* involved allegations of a number of *separate* incidents of rape (or attempted rape). The position will be different if it can be shown that the allegations are *connected* in some way. For example, in *Knutzen* v *Mauritzen* (1918), the pursuer had purchased 20 barrels of salt mutton, and brought an action against the seller for breach of contract, arguing that the mutton was putrid. In support of his case, he sought to prove that mutton purchased from the same consignment by another firm was also putrid. Lord Sands rejected the argument that this was a collateral issue into which the court should not enquire, observing (at 87–88) that:

> "I accept [counsel's] contention that the Court is not to be led into an enquiry into ulterior issues, merely because the facts averred might, if proved, have some slight significance as bearing upon the issue here to be tried. I am not able, however, in the present case to regard the significance as being necessarily slight. Where there is a dispute as to what was the quality or condition of certain goods of a homogeneous character, I think it may throw most important light upon the matter to ascertain the quality or condition of another parcel of goods from the same consignment. I do not therefore see how the pursuer can be denied an opportunity of proving that other barrels taken at random from the same lot were found to be putrid, any more than the defender could be denied an opportunity of proving that barrels which he did not send to the pursuer were, on examination, found to be in good condition."

Similarly, in *William Alexander & Sons Ltd* v *Dundee Corporation* (1950), an action arising out of a road accident in which it was alleged that the road had not been properly maintained, it was held to be relevant to lead evidence of previous accidents on the road.

Essential Facts

- Evidence which has little bearing on the case in hand may be held inadmissible on the basis that it relates to a "collateral issue", rather than to the facts which have to be decided by the court.

- This operates principally to exclude character evidence.

- Prior conduct of the accused, even where it indicates criminal activity with which he is not now charged, may be admissible if it is relevant to prove the offence with which he is charged (as opposed to simply undermining his credibility).

- There is a general prohibition against leading evidence of an accused person's prior convictions or of his bad character generally, except where:
  - it is relevant evidence to show that he is guilty of the offence with which he is charged;
  - the accused has put his own character or the character of prosecution witnesses in issue [but here the court has a discretion not to permit such evidence to be led despite the condition being satisfied];
  - the accused has given evidence against any other person charged in the same proceedings.

- Evidence of the character of a victim or complainer is generally inadmissible, but two cases require special consideration:
  - *Crimes of violence*: where self-defence is pled, it may be relevant to show that the victim or complainer had a violent temperament, but not (normally) to prove specific acts of violence committed by that person.
  - *Sexual offences*: evidence of the sexual history of a complainer is normally prohibited, but the accused may apply to lead such evidence or question the complainer on such matters if narrow statutory criteria are satisfied.

- The character of a witness (in both civil and criminal cases) may be challenged in cross-examination, but it is not normally competent to lead evidence of their character.

- Where, however, a witness is alleged to have made a prior statement which is inconsistent with their testimony in court, evidence may be led of the content of that statement. In criminal cases, however, evidence of the statement is admissible only for the purpose of discrediting the witness, and not as proof of the facts with which it is concerned.

- Collateral evidence is generally inadmissible in civil proceedings. However, evidence of matters sufficiently connected to the facts in dispute may be admissible.

Essential Cases

A v B (1895): where A brought an civil action alleging that B had raped her, she was not permitted to lead evidence of two separate allegations of attempted rape made against B by other women.

DS v HM Advocate (2007): the statutory rule that, where a person charged with a sexual offence is permitted to ask questions about the complainer's sexual history, his previous convictions can then be taken into account by the court (unless this is contrary to the interests of justice) is not contrary to the European Convention on Human Rights.

Gallagher v Paton (1909): where a person was charged with fraud, it was permissible to lead evidence of similar false statements which he had made earlier that day.

HM Advocate v Kay (1970): where a woman was charged with murdering her husband, on a libel which alleged that she had previously evinced malice and ill-will towards him, fairness required that she should be entitled to lead evidence of specific assaults by her on him. This is considered an exception to the normal rule that evidence of specific acts of violence by the (alleged) victim of a crime of violence is inadmissible.

Knutzen v Mauritzen (1918): where a purchaser alleged that mutton which they had bought was putrid, it was permissible to lead evidence showing that other mutton from the same consignment was also found by a separate purchaser to be putrid.

Leggate v HM Advocate (1988): accusing a Crown witness of lying is not in itself sufficient to trigger the statutory provisions allowing evidence of the accused's bad character to be admitted, or for the accused to be cross-examined on his character. Where the accused's defence goes further than this – for example, accusing Crown witnesses of conspiring to make false allegations against him – then the statutory provisions are triggered, although the court has a discretion not to permit character evidence to be admitted, or the accused being cross-examined in this way.

James Ritchie and Andrew Morren (1841): where two men were charged with passing false coins off as genuine, evidence to show they had unsuccessfully attempted to do this on a number of earlier occasions was held admissible.

10 PRIVILEGE

Privilege may arise as an objection to certain evidence being led, but it may also form the basis for one party seeking to prevent another from obtaining copies of otherwise relevant documents etc from them by way of pre-trial procedure (usually "commission and diligence"). Many, if not most, of the reported cases on privilege are concerned with such pre-trial procedure rather than admissibility at trial. This depends on the privilege in question, though: the privilege against self-incrimination is more likely to arise in the form of an objection to certain questions being asked at a trial or proof.

It may be helpful at the outset to distinguish "mere" confidentiality from privilege. Many communications may be regarded as confidential, in that a party to the communication can legally prevent the other from disclosing the communication, or take action in delict if it is unlawfully disclosed. However, unless the communication is also privileged, there is nothing to prevent evidence of its content being led in court (or to prevent the court compelling disclosure as part of pre-trial procedure).

So, for example, the doctor–patient relationship is regarded in law as confidential, but a doctor cannot refuse to give evidence about his patient (*AB* v *CD* (1851)). Similarly, a journalist cannot refuse to give evidence about a confidential source (*HM Advocate* v *Airs* (1975)). (However, in order for a journalist to be compelled to disclose the source of his information, disclosure must now be necessary in the interests of justice, national security or the prevention of disorder or crime: Contempt of Court Act 1981, s 10.)

In *Airs*, the appeal court did say (at 70) that "there remains a residual discretion in the Court to excuse a witness, who seeks to be excused upon a ground of conscience, from answering a relevant question in accordance with his legal duty". It appears that this discretion was used in an unreported case (*HM Advocate* v *Daniels* (1960)) to excuse a priest from giving evidence of matters relayed to him at confession. This discretion may, in exceptional cases, provide some protection where privilege is inapplicable.

The courts have not always been consistent on matters of terminology, and have frequently referred – for example – to solicitor–client "confidentiality". However, it is clear that the protection afforded to solicitor–client communications is much stronger than the ordinary protection of confidentiality, and so it is convenient to use the term "privilege" to denote the special protection given to such communications.

This chapter outlines the various types of privilege recognised by Scots law, including the analogous claim of public interest immunity.

The privilege against self-incrimination

A person cannot be obliged to answer a question if the answer might incriminate him by tending to show that he was guilty of a criminal offence (*Livingstone* v *Murrays* (1830)). However, the privilege applies only if the accused could potentially be prosecuted for the offence, and so cannot be claimed if he has already been tried or has been granted immunity from prosecution (*O'Neill* v *Wilson* (1983)). If an accused chooses to waive the privilege and admit a crime, he cannot thereafter decline to answer questions on points of detail (*Greenan* v *HM Advocate* (2007)).

A witness is also entitled to refuse to answer a question if the answer might tend to show that he has committed adultery (*Stephens* (1839); Evidence (Further Amendment) (Scotland) Act 1874, s 2). This rule was abolished in England as far back as 1968 (Civil Evidence Act 1968, s 16(5)).

Marital communications

Until recently, communications made between a husband and wife during their marriage were considered privileged in both criminal and civil proceedings. The privilege has now been abolished in criminal proceedings (Criminal Justice and Licensing (Scotland) Act 2010, s 86). It remains in existence in civil proceedings, however (Evidence (Scotland) Act 1853, s 3).

Legal professional privilege

Communications between a solicitor and a client are regarded as privileged, and therefore immune from disclosure in court. It is not just the content of the communication which is privileged: the mere identity of the client is also privileged (*Conoco (UK) Ltd* v *The Commercial Law Practice* (1997)). It is not restricted to discussions between a solicitor and a client regarding litigation, but applies to all communications between a solicitor and a client "although they may not relate to any suit depending or contemplated or apprehended" (*McCowan* v *Wright* (1852), per Lord Wood at 237).

The privilege belongs to the client, and so may be waived if the client chooses to do so. It is not clear how it is affected by the death of either the solicitor or the client, although it is thought that (if the solicitor dies) the solicitor's successors continue to be under an obligation of confidentiality and (if the client dies) the privilege may continue to be asserted by his solicitor or executors. (For further discussion, see *Walkers on Evidence* (3rd edn, 2009), para 10.2.3.)

What if no solicitor–client relationship is formed?

In *HM Advocate* v *Davie* (1881), a trial before the High Court on circuit, a potential client (Davie) consulted a solicitor about a civil action, but the solicitor declined to act for him. Davie was later prosecuted for perjury in respect of the civil action and the solicitor was called as a witness. The trial judge admitted the evidence, but on the basis that the point could be reconsidered by the High Court in Edinburgh. This proved unnecessary, because the charge against Davie was found not proven by the jury.

Davie remains the only Scots law authority on communications *in contemplation* of establishing a solicitor–client relationship. Insofar as it suggests that such communications are not privileged, it has been criticised repeatedly, and the better view may be that such communications should be regarded as privileged.

Fraud or other illegality

Privilege may be excluded where it is alleged that the solicitor has been directly concerned in fraud or another illegal act by the client. In *Micosta SA* v *Shetland Islands Council* (1983), the pursuers in an action against a local authority sought a court order to recover letters between the local authority and their legal advisers, arguing that because they were alleging an illegal act on the part of the authority, the communications were relevant to the intention or state of mind of the authority at the relevant time and so should not be regarded as privileged. The Inner House rejected this argument, saying (at 485): "So far as we can discover from the authorities the only circumstances in which the general rule will be superseded are where fraud or some other illegal act is alleged against a party and where his law agent has been directly concerned in the carrying out of the very transaction which is the subject-matter of inquiry."

The illegality exception was extended slightly in *Conoco (UK) Ltd* v *The Commercial Law Practice* (1997), where a firm of solicitors wrote to Conoco stating that their client – who they did not identify – had information regarding a fraud committed on the company by another person, and was prepared to divulge details in return for 20 per cent of the money that Conoco recovered. Conoco responded by bringing a court action for an order compelling the solicitors to disclose the identity of their client. Lord

Macfadyen granted the order, holding that although neither the solicitors nor their client were guilty of a fraud, they were seeking to benefit from the fraud of another, and so public policy considerations meant that the client's identity could not be regarded as privileged.

Privileges in aid of litigation

Communications post litem motam

Privilege attaches to communications made in contemplation of litigation, which are described as communications *post litem motam*. This privilege is not restricted to (or even concerned with) communications between a solicitor and a client – such communications are *always* protected by legal professional privilege. Instead, it applies to communications more generally – for example, letters between the solicitor (or the client) and an expert from whom a report is sought. In *Anderson* v *St Andrew's Ambulance Association* (1942), the Lord President (Normand) described the "general rule" as follows (at 557): "no party can recover from another material which that other party has made in preparing his own case".

It follows from this that communications and reports which are not made in contemplation of litigation will not be covered by privilege. However, the Inner House said in *More* v *Brown & Root Wimpey Highland Fabricators Ltd* (1983) (at 671) that "in the interests of certainty it must now be recognised that confidentiality ought to attach to all records and reports of investigations made after an accident has occurred". In such cases, there will be no room for an argument that litigation was not in contemplation at the time the record or report was made. (Cf *Marks & Spencer* v *British Gas Corporation* (1983), where a contrary view was taken, but this was a decision of a single judge.)

The rule outlined in *More* v *Brown and Root* does not apply to a report made to an employer by an employee present at the time of an accident, made at or about the time of the accident (*Young* v *National Coal Board* (1957)).

Communications in aid of negotiation

In practice, communications between parties who are attempting to reach a negotiated settlement may state that they are written "without prejudice" in an attempt to prevent them being relied upon by the other party at a later stage. It has sometimes been suggested that a letter written "without prejudice" cannot be used in evidence without the consent of both parties (see *Bell* v *Lothiansure Ltd* (1990)), but it is now doubtful that the words have such a special effect. In *Daks Simpson Group v Kuiper* (1994), Lord Sutherland considered a letter between two parties who sought to negotiate a settlement, which concluded with the words "without prejudice". He concluded that where a party had made a "clear and unequivocal admission of fact", there was nothing to prevent that admission being used in subsequent proceedings. The letter had stated that the defender was "prepared to accept" certain specific figures as being accurate, and this could be taken as an admission.

In *Richardson v Quercus Ltd* (1999), the Inner House suggested that *Daks* did not lay down an absolute rule, that each situation had to be judged on its own facts, and that the phrase "without prejudice" (or, perhaps better, "without prejudice to liability") might have a protective effect in appropriate cases. However, the cases indicate that "without prejudice" cannot be relied upon as guaranteeing that communications will be immune from future use in litigation. Accordingly, it is important to ensure that admissions of fact are not rashly made and are, where appropriate, expressly stated to be hypothetical positions which a party might be prepared to adopt for the purposes of settlement only.

Privileged communications obtained by a third party

If a privileged communication – or a copy of one – is obtained by a third party, is this admissible in evidence? (The problem only arises in respect of solicitor–client privilege and communications *post litem motam*; it will nor arise in respect of communications in aid of negotiation or settlement, which are deliberately made to the opposing party.)

The only Scottish authority appears to be *McLeish v Glasgow Bonding Company Ltd* (1965), where the defenders in a civil action had inadvertently obtained a copy of a privileged letter from the pursuer's solicitors to a potential medical witness. This letter would normally have been protected as a communication *post litem motam*, but it was held that since the defenders had obtained it without acting improperly or illegally, they were entitled to use it in evidence when cross-examining a witness for the pursuers. Lord Cameron, who heard the case, explicitly reserved his opinion as to whether his decision would have been the same had the letter been one between the *client* and the solicitors, where solicitor–client privilege would have applied.

McLeish aside, the point is regarded as unsettled. Two observations may be made. First, a privileged communication obtained by a third party is probably subject to the normal rules applying to improperly obtained real and documentary evidence, and Lord Cameron explicitly referred to those rules in deciding *McLeish*. The courts are reluctant to exclude relevant evidence in civil cases on the basis that it has been improperly obtained, but are likely to take a firmer line in criminal matters. (The rules on improperly obtained real and documentary evidence are set out in Chapter 8.) A second (and related) argument is that privilege is a rule which prevents certain individuals from disclosing protected information, rather than a rule as to the admissibility of evidence (as suggested in the English case of *R* v *Tompkins* (1978)). If that is the case, then once an item has been obtained by a third party, the relevant protection – if any – lies in the rules on improperly obtained evidence and not in the rules on privilege.

Public interest immunity

In some circumstances, it may be argued that items are immune from disclosure, or inadmissible as evidence, because of reasons of public policy. This is often referred to as "public interest immunity", although that is a term used in English law which has not been firmly established in Scotland.

Who can claim public interest immunity?

In *Higgins* v *Burton* (1968), Lord Avonside suggested that public interest immunity could only be claimed by a Minister of the Crown or the Lord Advocate, a suggestion repeated by Lord Sutherland in *P* v *Tayside Regional Council* (1989). It is not clear whether this remains the case, and the courts have occasionally been willing to consider such claims when made by other parties (see, for example, the claim made by a local authority in *McLeod* v *British Railways Board* (1997), although the claim was rejected). In England, by contrast, it is settled that claims of public interest immunity can be made by any party, and that the judge might even raise the issue if no party to the action does so (*R* v *Lewes Justices, ex parte Home Secretary* (1973)). The Scottish courts seem to have moved towards this position in *Al-Megrahi* v *HM Advocate* (2008), where the High Court held that a plea of public interest immunity (made on behalf of the UK Government by the Advocate General for Scotland) could be considered by the court even though the Lord Advocate herself had not pressed the point. In reaching that conclusion, the court referred, seemingly with approval, to Lord Reid's suggestion in *Lewes Justices* (at 400) that "it must be open to any person interested to raise the question").

The basis for the claim

In England, the courts at one time took the view that a claim of public interest immunity by a Minister was conclusive (*Duncan v Cammell Laird & Co Ltd* (1942)), but have now rejected this view (*Conway v Rimmer* (1968)). In Scotland, the courts never took this view and have always asserted the power to disregard the Minister's (or Lord Advocate's) objection (*Glasgow Corporation v Central Land Board* (1956)).

If a claim of public interest immunity is challenged, the court will have to balance the public interest in non-disclosure against the interests of the individual seeking the information – interests which will be particularly strong where the material is sought to assist the defence in a criminal trial.

A distinction has been drawn between a "class" and a "contents" claim to public interest immunity. The former involves a claim that there is an entire class of documents which must, in the public interest, remain immune from disclosure. The latter involves a claim that the contents of specific documents ought not to be disclosed for reasons of public interest. "Class" claims are now regarded as weak and difficult to establish. In *McLeod v HM Advocate* (1998), the Crown accepted that it could no longer claim that statements taken by the police from witnesses to crime attracted "class" immunity, but would instead have to establish specific grounds relating to the statement in question if they wished to argue it was immune from disclosure.

In the Scott Inquiry into the sale of arms to Iraq, the use of public interest immunity certificates came under particular scrutiny, because Ministers had attempted to use public interest immunity to prevent certain evidence being used at the criminal trial of individuals accused of breaching export guidelines, a trial which had collapsed after the judge ordered disclosure of some of the material concerned. After Sir Richard Scott's report was published, the Government made statements in Parliament indicating that it would no longer seek to claim public interest immunity unless disclosure of the particular documents concerned would cause serious harm to the public interest. (See I Dennis, *The Law of Evidence* (3rd edn, 2007), para 9.27, who notes that this "effectively abandons the contents/ class distinction".)

Essential Facts

- Where a communication is regarded as privileged, a party cannot be forced to disclose it for the purposes of litigation.
- A person cannot be obliged to answer a question if the answer might incriminate him as being guilty of a crime. This does not apply if he has already been tried for the crime or has been granted immunity from prosecution.
- Communications between a husband and wife, while married, are considered to be privileged even if they have since divorced.
- Communications between a solicitor and client are regarded as privileged, even if they do not relate to litigation.
- There is an exception to solicitor–client privilege where the solicitor is alleged to have been involved in an illegal act committed by the client, or where the solicitor is assisting a client to benefit from an illegal act committed by a third party.
- Communications made in contemplation of litigation – "communications *post litem motam*" – are regarded as privileged. This might include, for example, reports solicited from potential expert witnesses.
- Communications made in an attempt to negotiate a settlement have been suggested to be protected from use in court where written "without prejudice", but it now appears that a clear admission of fact in the communication is admissible in evidence against its maker even where the "without prejudice" phrase is used.
- Where a privileged communication falls into the hands of a third party, privilege will not necessarily prevent it being used as evidence, but the law is unsettled.
- In some circumstances, evidence may be inadmissible – or immune from disclosure – because "public interest immunity" applies: that is, it is in the public interest that the material should be immune from disclosure.
- The courts are not bound by a claim of public interest immunity and can choose to reject it.

Essential Cases

Al-Megrahi v HM Advocate (2008): a claim of public interest immunity can be considered by the courts even though it is not made by the Lord Advocate.

Anderson v St Andrew's Ambulance Association (1942): there is a general rule that "no party can recover from another material which that other party has made in preparing his case". Such communications are communications *post litem motam*.

Daks Simpson Group v Kuiper (1994): the fact that a communication is written "without prejudice" does not prevent a party from relying on clear and unequivocal admissions of fact contained within that communication.

Glasgow Corporation v Central Land Board (1956): the court is not obliged to uphold a claim of public interest immunity made by a Minister of the Crown or the Lord Advocate.

McLeish v Glasgow Bonding Company Ltd (1965): where the defenders in a civil action had inadvertently obtained a copy of a privileged communication written by the pursuer's solicitors, they were not prohibited from using it in cross-examination of the pursuer's witnesses.

Micosta SA v Shetland Islands Council (1983): solicitor–client communications may not be privileged where a party is alleged to have carried out an unlawful act and his solicitor has been directly concerned in carrying it out. In *Conoco (UK) Ltd v The Commercial Law Practice* (1997), this was extended slightly to cover the case of a solicitor whose client sought to benefit from the fraud of another.

11 OPINION EVIDENCE

This chapter outlines the general prohibition on the use of opinion evidence and the exceptions to that prohibition. The prohibition (and most of the exceptions) are common to both criminal and civil cases.

The general prohibition on opinion evidence

Witnesses should normally be asked to give evidence only on facts within their own knowledge, and not to give evidence of their opinion. For example, a witness to a road traffic accident – whether the matter forms the basis for action in a civil or criminal court – may give evidence describing the facts which he saw. He may not, however, give evidence as to who was to blame, or whether (supposing that the driver is charged with the offence of dangerous driving) he personally thought that the driving was "dangerous".

In some circumstances, however, it can be difficult to distinguish evidence of fact from evidence of opinion. Where a witness gives evidence of identification this might be termed an expression of opinion rather than an expression of fact. It is nevertheless accepted as being admissible (see, eg, *HM Advocate* v *Ronald* (2007)). It is also accepted that a witness may give evidence of "the impression produced on his mind at the time by what he observed" (Dickson, *A Treatise on the Law of Evidence in Scotland* (3rd edn, 1887), para 392). For example, it was held in *King* v *King* (1842) that, where a witness in a divorce case had observed one of the parties and her alleged lover together, she was entitled to give evidence of whether, at the time, she had formed the impression that intercourse had taken place.

The most important exception to the prohibition on opinion evidence is the use of "skilled" or "expert" witnesses. Dickson describes this exception as follows:

> "Another exception to the general rule against examining witnesses on matter of opinion, occurs wherever the issue involves scientific knowledge, or acquaintance with the rules of any trade, manufacture, or business, with which men of ordinary intelligence are not likely to be familiar." (*A Treatise on the Law of Evidence in Scotland* (3rd edn, 1887), para 397)

The rest of this chapter outlines the extent to which such "expert evidence" is permissible.

Who can be an expert witness?

Before a witness offers expert opinion in evidence, their qualifications to give such evidence must be established. This will normally be done simply by questioning the witness on the point and asking them to state their qualifications.

Often, such qualifications will be formal, such as degrees or membership of professional bodies. However, it is not essential that an expert has formal qualifications in the area on which they are giving evidence, provided that the court is satisfied they can in fact legitimately claim expertise in the area. For example, it was held in *Wilson* v *HM Advocate* (1988) that police officers and forensic scientists could competently give evidence about how cannabis oil was commonly imported into the country, a topic with which they were familiar through attending seminars and discussing drug enforcement questions with Customs and Excise officers.

An expert witness may legitimately refer to published literature when giving evidence, even if it is not strictly within his own field of expertise. An example is *Main* v *McAndrew Wormald Ltd* (1988), where medical witnesses made extensive reference to epidemiological literature when giving evidence. It was held that it was legitimate for them to do so, even although they were not themselves epidemiologists. Where an expert witness adopts passages in a published work, they become part of his evidence. Other passages (or other publications entirely) may be put to him in cross-examination, but if they are not put into evidence then the court cannot rely on them in order to displace or criticise his testimony (*Davie* v *Magistrates of Edinburgh* (1953)).

Establishing the factual basis for the expert evidence

If an expert witness is to give an opinion based on certain facts, those facts must be established in evidence.

For example, in *Stewart* v *Glasgow Corporation* (1958), a woman's child had been killed by an accident involving the breaking of a clothes-pole in October 1953. In an action for damages, she led evidence from two expert witnesses who said that, on the basis of the pole's condition in January 1954, it must have been visibly and dangerously corroded as far back as May 1953. However, only one of those witnesses had actually inspected the pole in January 1954 (the second expert based his opinion on the report by the first). Because, at the time, corroboration was required in all civil cases, this meant that the pursuer had not led sufficient evidence to prove the condition of the pole in January. Accordingly, the conclusions which the experts sought to draw as to the condition of the pole in May were valueless, as there was no factual basis for them.

In *Forrester* v *HM Advocate* (1952), expert evidence was led regarding the examination of a piece of cotton allegedly found in the accused's pocket, which it was said corresponded with a cotton bedspread used to commit the crime. However, the source of the piece of cotton examined by the expert witness was not proved in court. Accordingly, it was held that the expert evidence should not have been taken into consideration by the jury. The difficulties which arose in this case are now partially alleviated by s 68 of the Criminal Procedure (Scotland) Act 1995. Under that provision, where a witness is to give evidence as to a production he has examined, it is not necessary to prove that the production he examined is the one of which the police or procurator fiscal took possession, unless the accused gives advance notice that he does not admit this to be the case.

Does expert evidence require corroboration?

It was suggested in *Davie* v *Magistrates of Edinburgh* (1953) (per the Lord President (Cooper) at 39) that expert evidence did not require corroboration. However, this view was later rejected in *McKillen* v *Barclay Curle & Co Ltd* (1967).

In civil cases, the matter is now largely academic as the corroboration rule has been abolished (Civil Evidence (Scotland) Act 1988, s 1), but it is still crucial in criminal cases (see Chapter 4). It must be remembered that the corroboration rule does not require the evidence of every witness to be corroborated. What it requires is that there are two sources of evidence in respect of each "crucial fact". If an expert witness is simply expressing a view on how facts are to be *interpreted*, then corroboration may be unnecessary, or may be found in evidence which does not come from an expert witness.

Matters on which expert evidence is inadmissible

An expert witness will not be allowed to usurp the function of the judge or jury. In *Davie* v *Magistrates of Edinburgh* (1953), the Lord President (Cooper) described the duty of the expert witness as follows (at 40):

> "to furnish the Judge or jury with the necessary scientific criteria for testing the accuracy of their conclusions, so as to enable the Judge or jury to form their own independent judgment by the application of these criteria to the facts proved in evidence ... the bare *ipse dixit* [unsupported assertion] of a scientist, however eminent, upon the issue in controversy,

will normally carry little weight, for it cannot be tested by cross-examination nor independently appraised, and the parties have invoked the decision of a judicial tribunal and not an oracular pronouncement by an expert".

Accordingly, expert witnesses are prohibited from expressing opinions on questions of ordinary human nature and behaviour (which is taken to be within the knowledge of the court), or on the actual issue which the court has to decide.

Ordinary human nature and behaviour

An expert witness may not give evidence on ordinary matters of human nature and behaviour. In the English case of *R* v *Turner* (1975), Lawton LJ explained the rationale for this prohibition as follows (at 841): "[t]he fact that an expert witness has impressive scientific qualifications does not by that fact alone make his opinion on matters of human nature and behaviour within the limits of normality any more helpful than that of the jurors themselves; but there is a danger that they may think it does".

In *HM Advocate* v *Grimmond* (2002), a man was charged with sodomy against two young boys, who had made allegations against him in "stages" – first alleging indecent behaviour (which he had admitted) and only later making further, more serious, allegations. The Crown sought to lead expert evidence from a psychologist to show that a victim of sexual abuse might well disclose details of the abuse in stages in this way. This evidence would potentially have bolstered the credibility of the complainers' evidence. The trial judge, Lord Osborne, refused to admit the evidence, observing (at 512) that:

> "It might be that, if it were established that a witness suffered from some form of mental illness which was relevant to a consideration of the quality of the evidence of that witness, psychiatric evidence concerning the implications of the illness might be admissible. However, in the present case, there is no suggestion that either of the children who are the complainers in this case is other than an ordinary and normal child. That being so, it appears to me that the assessment of their credibility is exclusively a matter for the jury, taking into account their experience and knowledge of human nature and affairs."

Where it appears that a witness is not, to use Lord Osborne's terminology, an "ordinary and normal person", then expert evidence may be admissible to help the court assess the credibility and reliability of their testimony. See, for example, *Green* v *HM Advocate* (1983) (where psychiatric evidence that a complainer in a rape case was liable to fantasise and have delusions was admitted).

A related rule is the prohibition of "oath-helping", which means that it is not normally permissible to lead expert evidence to enhance the credibility of one's own witness. However, it was held in *HM Advocate* v *A* (2005) that, where the defence had been permitted to lead expert evidence which was adverse to the credibility of prosecution witnesses, principles of fairness meant that the defence could not rely on the rule against oath-helping to object to contrary expert evidence being led by the prosecution.

There is now a specific statutory provision permitting, in sexual offence cases, the use of expert psychological or psychiatric evidence "for the purpose of rebutting any inference adverse to the complainer's credibility or reliability which might otherwise be drawn from" behaviour or statements after the alleged offence. (Section 275C of the Criminal Procedure (Scotland) Act 1995, as inserted by s 5 of the Vulnerable Witnesses (Scotland) Act 2004.)

The "actual" or "ultimate" issue

In principle, a witness should not give evidence on the "actual issue" which the court has to decide. This is often referred to as the "ultimate issue" rule, although this terminology has not been used by the Scottish courts.

For example, in *Galletly* v *Laird* (1953), it was observed that, in a trial for obscenity, it would be inappropriate to ask a witness whether he considered the materials in question to be obscene, because the "purpose and effect" of such a question would be "to lay before the magistrate the opinion of a witness on the very matter remitted to the opinion of the magistrate" (per the Lord Justice-General (Cooper) at 27). Similarly, it was held in *Hendry* v *HM Advocate* (1987) that it was not permissible to ask an expert witness whether he believed that an essential fact – the cause of the victim's death – had been established "beyond reasonable doubt".

Although such evidence is in principle inadmissible, witnesses may in practice give evidence which comes very close to expressing an opinion on the actual issue before the court – and, indeed, a legitimate question which is not designed to elicit such evidence may inadvertently result in the witness giving an opinion on the point.

Furthermore, there is some evidence that the courts have been prepared to take a lax view of the prohibition against receiving evidence on the actual issue, particularly where medical or other scientific evidence is concerned. For example, it is clear that in trials for murder where the accused has pled the partial defence of diminished responsibility, medical witnesses have been asked directly and without objection whether they believed that the accused was suffering from diminished responsibility (see *Williamson* v *HM Advocate* (1994) and *Connelly* v *HM Advocate* (1991)). In the English case of *DPP* v *A & BC Chewing Gum Ltd* (1968), Lord Parker CJ observed (at 164) that "although technically the … question 'Do you think he was suffering from diminished responsibility?' is strictly inadmissible, it is allowed time and time again without any objection".

Essential Facts

- Witnesses should normally only give evidence of facts within their own knowledge. Accordingly, evidence of opinions is generally inadmissible.
- However, a witness can give evidence of the "impression produced on his mind at the time by what he observed".
- Expert witnesses may also give evidence of matters of opinion.
- An expert witness must have appropriate qualifications, although these need not be formal ones – relevant experience and knowledge will suffice.
- Where an expert witness is to give an opinion based on certain facts, those facts must be established in evidence.
- Expert witnesses cannot give evidence on matters of ordinary human nature and behaviour, nor on the "actual" or "ultimate" issue before the court.

Essential Cases

Davie v Magistrates of Edinburgh (1953): the function of an expert witness is to furnish the court with the necessary scientific criteria for testing the accuracy of their conclusions. They should not simply make unsupported assertions.

Galletly v Laird (1953): an expert witness could not be asked whether certain materials were "obscene", because that was the question which the court had to determine.

HM Advocate v Grimmond (2002): a psychologist could not give expert evidence about the way in which two young boys had disclosed allegations of sexual abuse – they were ordinary and normal children and this was a matter for consideration by the jury based on their own knowledge of human nature and affairs.

King v King (1842): a witness in a divorce case who had observed one of the parties and her alleged lover together could give evidence of whether she had, at the time, formed the impression that intercourse had taken place.

Wilson v HM Advocate (1988): police officers and forensic scientists could give evidence on how drugs were imported – they did not have formal qualifications on the topic but had acquired sufficient knowledge through their work.

12 JUDICIAL KNOWLEDGE

Judicial knowledge – or "judicial notice" – is a concept which allows courts to find certain facts (and matters of law) to be proven without the need for evidence to be led.

When a matter is within judicial knowledge, evidence of the matter is not only unnecessary but incompetent. So, for example, in *William Goodwin* (1837), a witness stated that a fact had happened on "Good Friday". The prosecution then attempted to lead evidence of the contents of an almanack to prove that Good Friday had fallen on the date libelled in the charge against Goodwin. The court held that this was incompetent – no explicit reasons were given, but it was presumably because the dates of the calendar are within judicial knowledge. This does not mean that the jury were expected to know the calendar by heart: the court held that they were entitled to see the almanack if they wished. This is consistent with the rule, explained below, that courts may refer to sources such as dictionaries and textbooks to establish facts said to be within judicial knowledge.

The fact that a matter is said to be within judicial knowledge does not necessarily mean that a judge will, in fact, be aware of it without counsel drawing it to the court's attention. For example, matters of law are generally said to be within judicial knowledge, but in *Glebe Sugar Refining Co Ltd* v *Greenock Harbour Trustees* (1921), it became clear during argument that the decision in the case turned on a statutory provision which had not been brought to the attention of the court (or the courts below). The Lord Chancellor (Lord Birkenhead) referred to the "extreme impropriety" of withholding relevant authority from the court, observing (at 74):

> "I myself find it very difficult to believe that some of those instructing learned counsel were not well aware of the existence, and the possible importance and relevance, of the section in question. It was the duty of such persons, if they were so aware, to have directed the attention of leading counsel to the section and to its possible relevance, in order that they in turn might have brought it to the attention of their Lordships."

As the above case makes clear, judicial knowledge is a legal concept and is not the same as the *personal* knowledge of a judge. For that reason, it was held in *Hattie* v *Leitch* (1889) that it was inappropriate for a judge to conduct a personal examination of a *locus*. However, it seems that judicial knowledge may vary from court to court, and so it was held in *Oliver* v

Hislop (1946) that a "Border sheriff" did not need to hear evidence on what a "cleek" – referred to in local regulations regarding salmon fishing – was.

Matters of law

The following matters of law are within judicial knowledge and do not require to be proved by evidence:

- Acts of the Westminster Parliament passed after 1850 (Interpretation Act 1978, s 3);

- Acts of the Scottish Parliament (Scotland Act 1998, s 28(6));

- European Community Treaties and the *Official Journal* of the European Communities (where Community legal instruments may be published) (European Communities Act 1972, s 3(2));

- Decisions of the Scottish courts and common law rules. This includes rules of customary international law, which it has been said form part of Scots law and therefore do not require to be proved by evidence (*Lord Advocate's Reference (No 1 of 2000)* (2001), per Lord Prosser at para 23).

It is thought that judicial notice will also be taken of Acts of Parliament prior to 1850 (including Acts of the old Parliaments of Scotland) and statutory instruments, but the position is not entirely clear (see *Walkers on Evidence* (3rd edn, 2009), paras 19.2.1 and 19.8.1). There are specific statutory provisions to facilitate the proof of statutory instruments and other subordinate legislation (including local byelaws) in criminal proceedings, allowing a copy to "be received as evidence of the due making, confirmation and existence of the order without being sworn to by any witness and without any further or other proof" (Criminal Procedure (Scotland) Act 1975, s 279A(3)).

As a matter of practice, notice may be taken of decisions of foreign courts as persuasive authority, but if foreign law is actually to be *applied* in a case before a Scottish court it must be proven as a matter of fact. However, it will be presumed that foreign law is identical to Scots law unless a difference is averred and proved (see, for example, *Rodden v Whatlings Ltd* (1961)) or admitted between the parties.

Matters of fact

Judicial notice of matters of fact takes two forms: notice without inquiry (also called notice of "notorious facts") and notice after inquiry.

There are some facts which are so well known – or "notorious" – that it would be pointless to debate them, one of the best-known examples being the fact that a fortnight is too short a period for human gestation (*R* v *Luffe* (1807)).

Elsewhere, a judge is entitled to have reference to sources such as dictionaries or textbooks in order to establish facts which are within judicial knowledge. (The list of appropriate sources is not limited to books: in *Duff Development Co* v *Government of Kelantan* (1924), it was held that a court could take judicial notice of the status of a foreign government – that is, whether it was an independent sovereign state – and that it was appropriate for the court to seek information from the Secretary of State as to whether this was the case.)

It is not possible to give a fixed list of facts which might be within judicial knowledge, either as notorious facts or after inquiry, but some examples can be given:

- Facts of history and public national events. See, for example, *MacCormick* v *Lord Advocate* (1953) (the proclamation of Queen Elizabeth as "Elizabeth the Second").
- Natural and scientific facts: see, for example, *McQuaker* v *Goddard* (1940) (the fact that camels are tame).
- The fact that a "Camic S" device was a device approved by the Secretary of State for testing the level of alcohol in a driver's breath: *Valentine* v *McPhail* (1986).

In *Doyle* v *Ruxton* (1999), it was suggested that it might be "a matter of judicial knowledge that well known brand names such as McEwan's Export, Guinness, Carlsberg Special Brew and the rest, are of such alcoholic strength that they can only be sold with an excise licence", although the court did not require to decide the point. The court distinguished the earlier case of *Grieve* v *Hillary* (1987), which involved "Schlitz" American beer – a brand "little known" in Scotland – meaning that without evidence as to its alcoholic content, the accused in that case could not be convicted of travelling on a prohibited coach on a passenger train with alcoholic liquor.

Essential Facts

- The concept of judicial knowledge allows courts to find certain facts (and matters of law) proven without the need for evidence to be led.
- The fact that a matter is "within judicial knowledge" does not necessarily mean that the court *will*, as a matter of practice, be aware of it – it may have to be drawn to the court's attention and the court may have to refer to appropriate sources such as textbooks to establish the point.
- Matters of law are generally within judicial knowledge and so do not require to be proved. This includes international and European law, but foreign law must be proved by evidence.
- Matters of fact may be within judicial knowledge if they are "notorious" or can be established by reference to appropriate sources such as textbooks.

Essential Cases

Glebe Sugar Refining Co Ltd v Greenock Harbour Trustees (1921): the parties to a case are obliged to bring relevant legal materials to the attention of the court.

Hattie v Leitch (1889): a judge should not have conducted a personal examination of a *locus*; judicial knowledge and personal knowledge are not the same thing.

13 JUDICIAL ADMISSIONS

Where a fact is "judicially admitted" by a party, it is not necessary to lead evidence to establish it. An admission only operates against the party making it – the pursuer in a civil action cannot, obviously, "admit" the defender's liability in any meaningful sense. Admissions may, however, be made by the parties jointly. This chapter sets out the relevant rules in civil and criminal cases.

Civil cases

In civil cases, "judicial admissions are in themselves, and without anything more, conclusive against the party making them, for the purposes of the action in which they are made" (*Walkers on Evidence* (3rd edn, 2009), para 11.2.1). This is not, however, always the case in family actions, the outcome of which – by determining questions such as marital status and parentage – may have consequences for persons who are not parties to the litigation. In such cases, specific provisions requiring evidence to be led often apply (for more detail, see *Walkers on Evidence* (3rd edn, 2009), para 27.2).

Admissions may be made in civil cases in one of four ways: (i) admissions in the closed record; (ii) minutes of admissions; (iii) notices to admit; and (iv) oral admissions at the bar.

Admissions in the closed record

The closed record is the final version of the written pleadings prepared by parties to a civil action. It will contain averments (claims of fact) by each party, some of which may be admitted by the other party. Where an averment is admitted, it has effectively been agreed between the parties and so it is unnecessary to lead evidence to prove the point.

It is only an admission of an averment that operates in this way. Where one party (A) makes an averment which is not admitted by the other party (B), B cannot then treat A's averment as an admission by A (*Lee v National Coal Board* (1955)).

An admission may be deleted before the record is closed (made final). In such a case, the admission no longer binds the party who originally made it. However, the other party may refer to the deleted admission in cross-examining witnesses led by the party who deleted it (*Lennox v National Coal Board* (1955)).

Minutes of admissions

The parties may jointly prepare a minute of admissions and lodge it with the court (or, indeed, a party might do so individually). While such a course may be competent and save on time and expense, it must be carefully undertaken:

> "In this case the parties elected to renounce probation [proof] upon an agreed joint minute of admissions in fact. This course has its advantages, but also its risks. The adjustment of such a minute is, in my judgment, one of the most difficult and delicate tasks which fall to the lot of counsel. An unguarded admission, or an inadvertent omission, may be fatal. But, once adjusted, the minute forms the evidence in the case; it is the proof at large, in synthesis; and its statement of admitted facts must be accepted as final."
> (*London & Edinburgh Steam Shipping Co* v *The Admiralty* (1920), per Lord Dundas at 318)

Notices to admit

These are governed by provisions in the Rules of the Court of Session (rr 28A.1–28A.2) and the sheriff court Ordinary Cause Rules (r 29.14). Under these provisions, it is possible for one party in a civil case to serve a "notice to admit" on the other party, calling upon them to admit specified facts. The other party may respond with a "notice of non-admission" within 21 days. If no such response is made, then he will be deemed to have admitted the facts specified in the notice to admit. However, the court may direct that the facts are not to be taken as admitted if "special cause" is shown.

Oral admissions at the bar

Oral admissions may be made by counsel or solicitors when appearing in court. Although this course is competent, if the admission is an important one it is preferable that it be put in writing, or that steps are taken to ensure that it is accurately recorded.

Criminal cases

In criminal cases, the only form of judicial admission recognised at common law is a plea of guilty which is accepted by the prosecutor. In *Strathern* v *Sloan* (1937), it was held that the prosecutor is not required to accept a plea of guilty, and may insist on the case going to trial. The court observed that there might be good reasons for refusing to accept a plea of guilty: perhaps in order to "bring out the full enormity of the crime", or where two persons were to be charged together and a trial was necessary "to assign the proper degree of guilt" to each of them. It is possible in certain circumstances to withdraw a plea of guilty, but not once a conviction has been recorded (*MacNeill* v *MacGregor* (1975)). It is, however, competent to appeal against a conviction based on a plea of guilty (*Boyle* v *HM Advocate* (1976)).

There is also statutory provision for admissions to be made in criminal cases. The first such provision is s 256 of the Criminal Procedure (Scotland) Act 1995, which provides that it "shall not be necessary for the accused or for the prosecutor ... to prove any fact which is admitted by the other", and allows the parties to agree the terms and application of documents. Admissions or agreements of evidence may be made by lodging a minute with the clerk of court. Under s 257 of the 1995 Act, the prosecutor and the accused are under a duty to seek the agreement of evidence, but the court has no explicit powers to take steps to enforce this duty.

The 1995 Act also makes provision, under s 258, in respect of "uncontroversial evidence". Here, one party in a criminal case can serve a notice on the other party (or parties) specifying facts which they consider are unlikely to be disputed. A party can challenge some or all of these facts, but if no challenge to the notice is made within 7 days, or only a partial challenge is made, then the unchallenged facts specified shall be deemed to be conclusively proved. The court can, however, direct that this deeming provision shall not apply if both parties agree or one party can point to "special circumstances" which mean that the facts in question should not be taken to be proved. Under a reform introduced by s 16 of the Criminal Procedure (Amendment) (Scotland) Act 2004, it is now theoretically possible for the court in solemn procedure to direct that a challenge is to be disregarded if it is considered "unjustified" (s 258(4A) of the 1995 Act), but it is not expected that this provision will be used widely, if at all.

There are also statutory provisions allowing for transcripts of police interviews and certificates as to forensic and scientific evidence to be taken as "sufficient evidence" of their contents (ss 277–284 of the 1995 Act). However, because such evidence is "sufficient" rather than "conclusive", it is open to the other party to dispute it at trial and lead contrary evidence.

Essential Facts

- Where a fact is judicially admitted by a party, it is not necessary to lead evidence to establish it.
- An admission operates only against the party making it.
- In civil cases, admissions may be made in one of four ways: (i) admissions in the closed record; (ii) minutes of admissions; (iii) notices to admit; and (iv) oral admissions at the bar.
- Where an admission is deleted from the record before it is closed (made final), it no longer binds the party who originally made it, but may be referred to in cross-examination.
- In criminal cases, the only form of judicial admission recognised at common law is a plea of guilty which is accepted by the prosecutor. The prosecutor is not required to accept a plea of guilty.
- Judicial admissions in criminal cases are now possible under statute.
- A party in a criminal case may serve a notice of "uncontroversial evidence". If the other party does not challenge the facts specified therein, they will be deemed to have been proved conclusively.

Essential Cases

Lee v National Coal Board (1955): where an averment is made in a closed record by one party (A), but is not admitted by the other party (B), B cannot treat the averment as an admission by A.

Lennox v National Coal Board (1955): where an admission is made in the record, but deleted before it is closed, it is no longer binding on the party who made it, but may be referred to in cross-examination.

Strathern v Sloan (1937): a prosecutor is never required to accept a plea of guilty, and may insist on the case going to trial.

14 *RES JUDICATA*

The plea of *res judicata* (literally, "thing decided") prevents parties from litigating the same matter twice. This might be regarded as part of the law of procedure rather than the law of evidence, but it is often covered in evidence courses and textbooks, and so is outlined briefly here.

Civil cases

The plea of *res judicata* in civil cases is generally described as having five elements (see *Walkers on Evidence* (3rd edn, 2009), para 11.5.1; Raitt, *Evidence* (2008), para 15.25). These are as follows:

(1) an earlier determination by a competent court or arbiter;

(2) that determination must have been pronounced "*in foro contentioso*" (a contested, rather than an undefended, case) without fraud or collusion;

(3) the prior determination must have concerned the same subject-matter;

(4) the grounds of action (*media concludendi*) must have been the same;

(5) the action must be between the same parties.

Criminal cases

A plea of *res judicata* in a criminal case may be founded on one of two different bases. These are: first, that the accused has previously stood trial on the same charge and been convicted or acquitted (sometimes referred to as "tholed assize") or, secondly, that the charge which the accused now faces has previously been held by a court to be incompetent or irrelevant.

The plea only applies where both sets of proceedings are concerned with the same crime. It is not enough that they both arise out of the same set of facts. There are a number of cases where an accused has been convicted (or acquitted) of assault and later charged with culpable homicide after the death of the victim: in such cases the courts have consistently held that culpable homicide and assault are not the same crime and so the plea does not apply. The leading case is *Isabella Cobb or Fairweather* (1836); see, more recently, *Tees* v *HM Advocate* (1994). On a similar basis, it was held in *HM Advocate* v *Cairns* (1967) that, after a man had been acquitted of murder and allegedly confessed thereafter to having committed the crime, it was competent to prosecute him for having committed perjury at his first trial.

Where a conviction is quashed on appeal, the appeal court now has the power to grant authority for a fresh prosecution (Criminal Procedure (Scotland) Act 1995, ss 118(1)(c) and 183(1)(d)). In such a case, the plea of *res judicata* will not be effective.

Successive civil and criminal cases

The plea of *res judicata* does not operate between civil and criminal cases: that is, the outcome of a civil case does not bar a subsequent criminal prosecution, and vice versa.

However, there are statutory provisions which allow for the fact of a criminal conviction to be admissible in civil proceedings (ss 10 and 12 of the Law Reform (Miscellaneous Provisions) (Scotland) Act 1968). Under s 10, where a person is proved to have been convicted of an offence before a United Kingdom court or court-martial, "he shall be taken to have committed that offence unless the contrary is proved". Under s 12, where the question of whether a person has committed a criminal offence is relevant to a defamation action, the conviction is *conclusive* evidence that he did indeed commit the offence.

Essential Facts

- The plea of *res judicata* prevents parties from litigating the same matter twice.
- In civil cases, the plea has five elements: (1) an earlier determination by a competent court or arbiter; (2) pronounced *in foro contentioso* without fraud or collusion; (3) concerning the same subject-matter; (4) the same grounds of action; (5) the same parties.
- In criminal cases, the plea requires that the crime charged in both proceedings is the same.
- Where a conviction is quashed on appeal, the court may authorise a retrial, in which case the plea of *res judicata* will not be effective.
- The plea of *res judicata* does not operate between civil and criminal cases, although criminal convictions may be relied upon as evidence in civil proceedings.

Essential Cases

HM Advocate v Cairns (1967): where a man was acquitted of murder but later allegedly confessed to the crime, it was competent to charge him with having committed perjury at his trial, as this was a different crime from murder.

Isabella Cobb or Fairweather (1836): where a woman was acquitted of assault but the victim later died, it was competent to charge her with murder on the basis that this was a different crime.

15 SPECIALITIES OF WITNESSES

This chapter considers rules which apply to particular types of witness, rather than the evidence which they may be called to give. Two concepts are crucial here. The first is *competence*: certain witnesses simply cannot be called to give evidence (or at least cannot be called by certain parties). The second is *compellability*: certain witnesses can competently give evidence, but cannot be required to do so.

This chapter also outlines special statutory provisions which apply to "vulnerable" witnesses, and briefly notes the position of anonymous witnesses.

The accused

At common law, an accused person could not competently give evidence at his own trial, a rule which was abolished by s 1 of the Criminal Evidence Act 1898 (see now s 266(1) of the Criminal Procedure (Scotland) Act 1995). It is now open to the accused to give evidence, but if he chooses to do so, he cannot refuse to answer questions on the basis that answering would tend to incriminate him as to the offence charged (s 266(3)).

The failure of the accused to give evidence can be commented on by the court or the prosecutor. (Comment by the prosecutor was formerly barred by statute, but this restriction was removed by s 32 of the Criminal Justice (Scotland) Act 1995.) Counsel for a co-accused can similarly comment (*Shevlin* v *HM Advocate* (2002)). In *Scott* v *HM Advocate* (1946), the Lord Justice-General (Normand) remarked that, while it was competent for the court to make such comment, "it should be made with restraint and only when there are special circumstances which require it". It seems that a prosecutor is subject to similar restraint, but – according to *Shevlin* – counsel for a co-accused is not.

A co-accused

An accused person is a competent witness for a co-accused, but is not compellable. Alternatively, if an accused person gives evidence on his own behalf, he may be cross-examined by a co-accused. One accused cannot, however, do both: that is, call a co-accused as a witness and cross-examine him when he gives evidence on his own behalf. (For these points, see s 266(9) of the Criminal Procedure (Scotland) Act 1995.)

Where a co-accused ceases to be an accused person (because he pleads guilty or is acquitted, or because the proceedings against him are deserted), he becomes a competent and compellable witness for either the prosecution or defence (s 266(10) of the 1995 Act).

Witnesses called by a co-accused

In *Todd* v *HM Advocate* (1984), it was argued that where a witness – who was not herself accused – gave evidence for one accused person, her evidence could not be used against that person's co-accused. The appeal court held that, even if this had been a rule in the past, it was not part of the modern law of evidence. Accordingly, evidence adduced on behalf of one accused could be evidence against his co-accused.

An accomplice (*socius criminis*)

It used to be said that, where an accomplice gave evidence against an accused person, the jury had to be given a special warning about the dangers of relying on such evidence (*Dow* v *McKnight* (1949)). However, it was decided in *Docherty* v *HM Advocate* (1987) that there was no rule that such a "*cum nota*" warning was required in all cases where an accomplice gave evidence, although it might be appropriate to give such a warning in some cases. In *Casey* v *HM Advocate* (1993), the appeal court said that a warning of this nature would have been inappropriate where the accomplice was also a co-accused and therefore entitled to the presumption of innocence.

Where the Crown calls a witness in order that he can admit his part in the criminal actions charged against another person (or persons), he acquires immunity from prosecution. A person in this position is sometimes referred to as a *socius criminis*. The reason for this rule is a practical one: unlike any other witness, "the *socius criminis* is called by the Crown for the express purpose of testifying that he was an accomplice in the crime charged. If he did not have the protection of immunity he would not be bound to answer any questions ..." (*O'Neill* v *Wilson* (1983), per the Lord Justice-General (Emslie) at 49). (This is because of the privilege against self-incrimination, discussed in Chapter 10.) By contrast, a Crown witness who admits to *other* criminal activity while giving evidence does not acquire immunity from prosecution as a result of such admissions (*O'Neill*).

The spouse of the accused

At common law, a spouse was not a competent witness at the trial of the other spouse, but by statute he or she is now a competent witness at the instance of either the prosecution or defence (Criminal Procedure (Scotland) Act 1995, s 264). Until recently, he or she was not a compellable witness for the prosecution unless he or she was the alleged victim of the crime (*Foster* v *HM Advocate* (1932)). By statute (Civil Partnership Act 2004, s 130), a similar rule applied in respect of civil partners.

The law was changed by s 86 of the Criminal Justice and Licensing (Scotland) Act 2010. As a result, spouses and civil partners are competent and compellable witnesses, except, of course, where they are themselves a co-accused with their spouse or partner and so entitled, like any other accused person, to refuse to give evidence.

Other relatives of the accused

Relatives of the accused, other than a spouse or civil partner, are competent and compellable witnesses for either the prosecution or the defence (Criminal Procedure (Scotland) Act 1995, s 265).

Persons present in court

At common law, a person who was present in court during the evidence of other witnesses was not a competent witness, except for expert witnesses who were permitted to hear other witnesses give factual evidence. Now, the matter is regulated by s 267 of the Criminal Procedure (Scotland) Act 1995, which provides that a court may permit a witness to be in court during the proceedings before he gives evidence if this "would not be contrary to the interests of justice" (s 267(1)). If a witness is present without the consent of the court or the parties to the proceedings, the court nevertheless has a discretion to permit him to give evidence (s 267(2)).

Court personnel

- *Judges* are competent witnesses (see, for example, *Davidson* v *McFadyen* (1942), where a sheriff – along with his clerk – gave evidence against a person who was accused of having committed perjury in his court). However, it appears that it is not competent to call a judge of the Court of Session or High Court to testify as to evidence which was given in court when he or she was presiding (*Muckarsie* v *Wilson* (1834)).
- *Prosecutors* cannot give evidence if they are personally conducting the prosecution (*Graham* v *McLennan* (1911)), but otherwise appear to be competent witnesses.

- *Defence agents* are competent witnesses, and in *Campbell* v *Cochrane* (1928) it was held permissible for a solicitor to conduct the defence in a criminal trial *and* tender himself as a witness. If an accused person chooses to call his present or former agent as a witness, he is not entitled to object to questions put to that witness on the ground of confidentiality (Criminal Procedure (Scotland) Act 1995, s 265(2)).

- *Jurors* cannot give evidence of their deliberations, because these are secret and cannot be investigated by a court or anyone else (*McGuire* v *Brown* (1963); Contempt of Court Act 1981, s 8). Otherwise, a juror should be a competent witness.

The competency of child witnesses

There is no specific age below which a child cannot give evidence in court, and the courts have been prepared to admit evidence from a child of as young as 3½ years old (*Janet Miller* (1870)). This was, however, formerly subject to a "competency test", whereby the court had to satisfy itself that the child knew the difference between truth and lies and then admonished the child to tell the truth. In *Quinn* v *Lees* (1994), the Lord Justice-General (Hope) outlined (at 161) which children were subject to this procedure and which children would simply take the oath in the same manner as adult witnesses:

> "A child who is under the age of twelve is not normally put on oath at all. He is admonished to tell the truth, after the [competency test] has been carried out. On the other hand, a child who is aged fourteen years or more is normally put on oath, and no question arises as to any preliminary procedure. Where a child is between the ages of twelve and fourteen the judge must satisfy himself that the child understands the nature of the oath. Unless he is so satisfied, it is not appropriate for him to put a child who is under the age of fourteen on oath."

The competency test is now, however, largely only of historic interest. It has been abolished by s 24 of the Vulnerable Witnesses (Scotland) Act 2004, which provides as follows:

> "(1) The evidence of any person called as a witness (referred to in this section as 'the witness') in criminal or civil proceedings is not inadmissible solely because the witness does not understand –
> (a) the nature of the duty of a witness to give truthful evidence, or
> (b) the difference between truth and lies.

(2) Accordingly, the court must not, at any time before the witness gives evidence, take any step intended to establish whether the witness understands those matters."

Although the competency test has been abolished, this does not affect the rules regarding oath or admonition, which remain as outlined in *Quinn* v *Lees*. (See *Walkers on Evidence* (3rd edn, 2009), para 13.3.2.)

Vulnerable witnesses

The process of giving evidence can be distressing for vulnerable witnesses, particularly in criminal proceedings. Accordingly, special provision is made for such witnesses by legislation, and these provisions have recently been overhauled by the Vulnerable Witnesses (Scotland) Act 2004, which makes extensive amendments to the Criminal Procedure (Scotland) Act 1995. Under this legislation, vulnerable witnesses may be entitled to the benefit of "special measures" when giving evidence in court.

The remainder of this section outlines the provisions of the statute in respect of criminal cases only, although parallel (but not exactly identical) provisions exist in respect of civil cases: see Pt 2 of the 2004 Act.

Who is a "vulnerable witness"?

A "vulnerable witness" is a person who falls into one of the following categories (s 271(1) of the Criminal Procedure (Scotland) Act 1995, as amended):

- a child witness (a person "under the age of 16 on the date of commencement of the proceedings in which the trial is being or to be held");
- a person who is not a child witness, but in respect of whom "there is a significant risk that the quality of the evidence to be given by the person will be diminished by reason of" (a) mental disorder or (b) "fear and distress in connection with giving evidence at the trial".

The accused themselves can be a vulnerable witness (see s 271F).

What special measures are available for vulnerable witnesses?

The following special measures are available to the court in respect of vulnerable witnesses (s 271H of the Criminal Procedure (Scotland) Act 1995, as amended):

- taking of evidence by a commissioner (which will be video recorded for use in the proceedings);
- giving evidence by a live television link;
- using a screen (which should conceal the accused from the sight of the witness, but be coupled with arrangements allowing the accused to see and hear the witness give evidence);
- using a supporter (a person who may be present alongside the witness when giving evidence, but must not prompt or seek to influence them);
- giving evidence in chief in the form of a prior statement. (Evidence "in chief" is that in response to initial questions from the party who calls the witness – the witness is still liable to cross-examination and, possibly, further questions by the party who calls him or her. The court can authorise the use of another special measure for these purposes.)

When should special measures be authorised?

Certain special measures are referred to as "standard special measures", a concept which applies in respect of child witnesses only. These are (a) giving evidence by a live television link; or (b) with the use of a screen; and (c) the use of a supporter in conjunction with either (a) or (b). Where a party calling a child witness requests that standard special measures be used, the court is obliged to grant the request. However, a party can also request that the child give evidence without the use of any special measures, which the court can authorise if satisfied that the child has expressed a wish to give evidence in this way and that it is appropriate for them to do so. (See s 271A of the Criminal Procedure (Scotland) Act 1995, as amended.) There are further protections for child witnesses under 12 in respect of sexual offences or offences of violence, under which the court should not normally require the witness to be in the court building for the purpose of giving evidence (s 271B).

In all other cases, the court has a discretion as to whether or not a special measure should be authorised in the circumstances (s 271C).

Anonymous witnesses

In *HM Advocate* v *Smith* (2000), it was held that undercover police officers could, if the accused's right to a fair trial would not be violated, be permitted to give evidence anonymously. Following the decision of the House of Lords in the English case of *R* v *Davis* (2008), where a conviction based on the evidence of anonymous witnesses was quashed on the basis that the right to a fair trial had been breached, a decision was taken to create a statutory regime governing the use of anonymous witnesses. A detailed statutory framework is now provided by ss 271N-271Z of the Criminal Procedure (Scotland) Act 1995, as inserted by s 90 of the Criminal Justice and Licensing (Scotland) Act 2010.

Essential Facts

- Certain persons may be regarded as not *competent* to give evidence – meaning that they simply cannot be called as witnesses; or as not *compellable* – meaning that they can be called as witnesses but cannot be required to give evidence.

- An accused person cannot be compelled to give evidence, but is a competent witness in his own defence.

- If an accused person does not give evidence, his failure to do so may be commented on by the court, the prosecutor or counsel for a co-accused.

- An accused person is a competent witness for a co-accused, but is not compellable.

- Where the Crown calls an accomplice – not himself charged with the crime – in the criminal activity alleged against those on trial, and does so in order that he can admit his part in the crime, he acquires immunity from prosecution. A person in this position is sometimes referred to as a *socius criminis*.

- The spouse of an accused is a compellable witness for the defence, but not for the prosecution – unless they are the alleged victim of the crime.

- Relatives of the accused other than a spouse (or civil partner, who is also not compellable) are competent and compellable witnesses for either the prosecution or defence.

- The court has a discretion to permit witnesses to be present in court, hearing other witnesses, before they themselves give evidence.

- Judges, prosecutors and defence agents are generally competent witnesses, subject to some exceptions.

- Jurors cannot give evidence of their deliberations but are otherwise competent witnesses.

- There is no minimum age below which a person cannot give evidence. Child witnesses were formerly subject to a "competency test" before giving evidence, but this has now been abolished by statute.

- Certain witnesses are regarded as "vulnerable" – children, persons suffering from mental disorder and persons whose evidence may be affected by "fear or distress". They are potentially entitled to "special measures" when giving evidence in criminal cases.

- "Special measures" include taking evidence by a commissioner, giving evidence by live television link, the use of a screen or supporter, or the use of a prior statement as evidence in chief.

- The court has a discretion as to whether or not special measures should be used when a vulnerable witness gives evidence, except that child witnesses are always entitled to "standard special measures" – either a television link or a screen, either of which may be combined with a supporter.

Essential Cases

Docherty v HM Advocate (1987): there is no rule that juries must always be given a special "*cum nota*" warning against relying on the evidence of an accomplice.

Scott v HM Advocate (1946): the court can comment on a witness's failure to give evidence, but such comment "should be made with restraint and only when there are special circumstances which require it".

Todd v HM Advocate (1984): it was argued that where a witness gave evidence for one accused person, her evidence could not be used against a co-accused. It was held that there is no such rule in the modern law of evidence.

16 THE CONDUCT OF A TRIAL OR PROOF

This chapter gives a very brief overview of how a trial (in criminal cases) or proof (in civil cases) will be conducted. It considers the following issues: first, "who leads?" – that is, which party must present their case first? Secondly, it outlines the rules relating to the questioning of witnesses, including the use of notes by witnesses to refresh their memory of events. Finally, it notes what should happen when an objection is made to certain evidence being admitted, and the potential consequences of failing to make an objection at the trial.

Who leads?

In criminal trials, the prosecution always leads. At the end of the prosecution case, it is open to the defence to make a submission of "no case to answer", claiming that the Crown has not led corroborated evidence which could establish that the accused has committed the crime charged – or, at least, an alternative charge of which he could be convicted (Criminal Procedure (Scotland) Act 1995, ss 97 and 160). If that submission is upheld, the accused will be acquitted immediately without the need to lead any evidence. Even if it is rejected, that only means that *sufficient* evidence has been led to convict the accused – even if the defence does not lead any evidence, it would still be open to the judge or jury to conclude that the case has not been proven beyond a reasonable doubt.

In civil cases, the pursuer will normally lead at the proof. Occasionally, however, it may be that the burden of proof lies on the defender and that it is appropriate for him to lead. An example is *Bishop* v *Bryce* (1910), where the defender in an action for payment of a debt admitted in the written pleadings that he had granted an IOU, but claimed that it was a temporary receipt and that the debt had been extinguished. It was held that the defender should lead at the proof, because the onus was on him to prove these claims.

Questioning witnesses: examination in chief, cross-examination and re-examination

The term "examination in chief" refers to the questioning of a witness by the party who has called him to give evidence. That witness may then be cross-examined by the other party (or parties) and thereafter "re-examined" by the party who called him, if that party so wishes.

(This should normally end the process, but if re-examination elicits new material from the witness, as opposed to merely clearing up ambiguities – the normal purpose of re-examination – further cross-examination may be permitted.)

Witnesses must take the oath or affirm to tell the truth before they give evidence. The standard forms of oath and affirmation are "I swear by Almighty God that I will tell the truth, the whole truth and nothing but the truth" and "I solemnly, sincerely and truly declare and affirm that I will tell the truth, the whole truth and nothing but the truth". The form of the oath may be amended if the witness's religious beliefs require it, although where the oath is taken its validity cannot be affected by the witness having had no religious belief (Oaths Act 1978, s 4(2)). Children under 14 may simply be admonished to tell the truth.

Failure to cross-examine

Criminal cases. A failure by the defence to cross-examine a Crown witness does not supply corroboration of the prosecution's case (*Wilson* v *Brown* (1947); *Morton* v *HM Advocate* (1938)). More generally, a failure to cross-examine a witness may be taken into account in weighing the evidence, but such failures do not amount to implied admissions of statements made in evidence in chief (*Young* v *Guild* (1985)).

Civil cases. In one case, it was suggested that a failure to cross-examine a witness for the defenders amounted to an implied admission that the contrary evidence given by the pursuers' witnesses had been discredited (*Keenan* v *Scottish Co-operative Wholesale Society Ltd* (1914)). However, the courts have not in modern practice taken such a harsh line, and it is now accepted that a failure to cross-examine a witness does not bar the court from rejecting their testimony (*Walker* v *McGruther & Marshall Ltd* (1982)).

If one party intends to lead evidence contradicting the other party's witness on a matter of fact, they should normally put the point to that witness in cross-examination. A failure to do so may leave them liable to expenses if the witness has to be recalled later, or, at worst, "cause fatal damage" to their case (*McKenzie* v *McKenzie* (1943), per the Lord Justice-Clerk (Cooper) at 109).

Leading questions

A leading question is one which suggests its own answer (for example, "Did you see Jimmy stab Bruce?" as opposed to "What did you see?"). These are permissible in cross-examination (except, perhaps, where the witness is in fact favourable to the party conducting the cross-examination).

During examination in chief and re-examination, by contrast, a party may not ask leading questions, except on matters which are uncontroversial (such as the name and address of a witness, or other matters which are not in dispute between the parties). However, it will occasionally happen that a witness proves "hostile", by giving evidence conflicting with that which he had previously indicated he would give, or by being reluctant to answer questions. In such circumstances, the witness may be treated as a "hostile witness", and questioned as if he were under cross-examination (*Brennan v Edinburgh Corporation* (1962), per Lord Sorn at 42). Because leading questions are permissible in cross-examination, they may therefore become legitimate in examination in chief – although the court may consider that answers elicited in this way carry less weight as evidence.

Other types of objectionable question

Two other types of question are commonly regarded as objectionable, at least in certain circumstances – first, hypothetical questions (those which put a hypothesis to the witness). These will generally be objectionable unless evidence to support the hypothesis has been or will be led, or if the question of what the witness might have done had circumstances been different is relevant to the case.

The second objectionable category is "double questions" – those which make an implied assertion. Dickson gives the example of asking "how much money was paid, when the witness has not stated that any payment was made" (*A Treatise on the Law of Evidence in Scotland* (3rd edn, 1887), para 1771).

Recalling witnesses and leading additional evidence

In some circumstances, it may be competent for a party to recall witnesses or lead additional evidence, as follows:

Recall of a witness. Where a witness has finished giving evidence, but before the party calling him has concluded that case, the party concerned may move to recall him to give further evidence (Evidence (Scotland) Act 1852, s 4 (civil proceedings); Criminal Procedure (Scotland) Act 1995, s 263(5) (criminal proceedings)). The judge has a discretion as to whether or not this motion should be granted.

Additional evidence. In criminal cases, there are statutory provisions which permit either party to move to lead "additional evidence" where this is *prima facie* material and was not available and could not reasonably have been made available at the commencement of the trial, or the party could not reasonably have foreseen that it would be material (Criminal Procedure (Scotland) Act 1995, s 268). Such a motion must be made before the commencement of speeches to the jury (in solemn procedure) or before the prosecutor proceeds to address the judge on the evidence (in summary procedure).

Proof in replication. In criminal cases, the prosecutor may move for a "proof in replication". This is permitted for two purposes only: either to contradict evidence given by a defence witness "which could not reasonably have been anticipated by the prosecutor", or to prove that a witness has on a specified occasion made a statement different from the evidence given by him at the trial (Criminal Procedure (Scotland) Act 1995, s 269). Such a motion must be made before the commencement of speeches to the jury (in solemn procedure) or before the prosecutor proceeds to address the judge on the evidence (in summary procedure).

In civil cases, proof in replication is competent where the party leading at the proof wishes to contradict evidence led by the other party which could not have been anticipated (*Walkers on Evidence* (3rd edn, 2009), para 12.4.1).

Refreshing memory

In giving evidence, a witness is entitled to refer to notes which he made at the time or shortly thereafter. The most common example is that of a police officer referring to a notebook when giving evidence. This is referred to as "refreshing memory", and its operation has been described as follows:

> "Notes taken by the observer of an event to which he speaks in the witness-box are not in themselves evidence in any sense. The evidence consists in the account given by the witness of what took place in his presence, and a note or jotting which he may have taken, on observing the facts to which he afterwards speaks, is in itself evidence of nothing. If, however, when he gives his evidence, he requires to look at the notes in order to enable him to give his account of what occurred, then the notes become part of his oral evidence. They are – so to speak – read into his oral testimony ..." (*Hinshelwood* v *Auld* (1926), per the Lord Justice-General (Clyde) at 7–8)

If a witness for one party uses notes in this way, the other party is entitled to see them. However, this right does not apply where the witness took notes at the relevant time but does not use them in giving evidence, and so there is no right for the accused to demand to see a policeman's notebook if he does not refer to it (*Hinshelwood* v *Auld* (1926); *Deb* v *Normand* (1997)).

A witness can only use notes to *refresh* memory. If he has no memory at all of the relevant events, he cannot use his notes as a substitute (*Angus McPherson* (1845)).

Objections to evidence

A party in a civil or criminal case may raise an objection to the admissibility of evidence which another party wishes to lead. The procedure for dealing with such objections differs between civil and criminal cases, as do the consequences of a failure to make an objection.

Criminal cases

Where evidence is objected to in a summary criminal case (where there is no jury), it was formerly suggested that the trial judge could hear the evidence "under reservation as to its admissibility" and decide at a later stage whether it was in fact admissible. It has now been held (in *Thompson* v *Crowe* (2000)) that this course is not appropriate and that the judge should decide the question of admissibility when the objection is made, after hearing evidence if necessary (a "trial within a trial"), which will be required if the facts as to the circumstances in which the evidence is obtained are in dispute. In solemn procedure, this process should take place outwith the presence of the jury.

Where an accused has been legally represented at trial, his conviction may not be quashed on appeal because of the admission of evidence which should have been rejected, unless his objection to the evidence was timeously stated at the trial (Criminal Procedure (Scotland) Act 1995, ss 118(8)(b)(ii) (solemn procedure) and 192(3)(b)(ii) (summary procedure)).

Civil cases

Where evidence is objected to in civil cases, it may be admitted "under reservation as to its admissibility", meaning that the judge can rule on its admissibility at a later stage. As in criminal cases, it is assumed that the judge will be able – if necessary – to disregard the inadmissible evidence in deciding the case and will not be prejudiced by having heard it. Although this procedure has been disapproved of in criminal cases (see above), it is explicitly sanctioned by the rules governing summary cause proceedings in the sheriff court (Summary Cause Rules, r 8.15).

As with criminal proceedings, such a course will not be appropriate in a civil case which is heard before a jury.

In civil cases, the issue of a failure to object to evidence has arisen less often in the reported cases, which is unsurprising given that the exclusionary rules are not as extensive as in criminal procedure. There are, however, a number of cases where one party has not objected to the leading of evidence which should have been inadmissible because it had no basis in the written pleadings (the "closed record"). In such cases, it has been held that the lack of an objection means that the evidence may be relied upon. (See, for example, *McGlone* v *British Railways Board* (1966).)

Essential Facts

- In criminal cases, the prosecution always leads at the trial. In civil cases, the pursuer will normally lead, but the defender may be required to lead if the burden of proof rests with him.

- Witnesses give evidence in three stages: examination in chief (questioning by the party calling them); cross-examination (questioning by the other party or parties); and re-examination (further questioning after cross-examination, to clear up ambiguities).

- Parties are not required to cross-examine witnesses called to give evidence against them, although it may harm their case if they do not do so. A failure to cross-examine, however, is not – at least normally – to be taken as an admission of the evidence elicited by examination in chief.

- Leading questions are regarded as inappropriate, except in cross-examination. Other inappropriate forms of questioning include double questions and (at least in some cases) hypothetical questions.

- In giving oral evidence, a party may refer to notes made at the time or shortly thereafter to refresh his memory. If he does so, they become part of his evidence and the other party is entitled to see them.

- If one party wishes to object to another leading inadmissible evidence, an objection should be made at the time. In criminal cases, if this is not done, the courts are statutorily barred from allowing an appeal on the basis that the evidence should not have been led.

Essential Cases

Hinshelwood v Auld (1926): a witness may refer to notes made at the time or shortly thereafter to refresh his memory, but if he chooses not to do this the other party may not demand to see his notes. Confirmed in *Deb* v *Normand* (1997).

Morton v HM Advocate (1938): a failure by the defence to cross-examine a prosecution witness does not amount to corroboration of that witness's evidence.

Walker v McGruther & Marshall Ltd (1982): a failure to cross-examine a witness in a civil case does not bar the court from rejecting their testimony.

INDEX

NOTES

NOTES

NOTES

NOTES

NOTES

NOTES

NOTES

NOTES